You live, you learn...

It's the refrain of one of Alanis Morissette's most popular hit singles—and anyone who's followed her career knows that it's much more than just a lyric. Writing songs at the age of nine, appearing on TV at ten, scoring a hit album and a major music award in her tender teens, Alanis had lived and learned plenty . . . and then, determined to cast off her false "disco diva" image and make her own music, she left for Los Angeles and learned much, much more. This fascinating biography reveals the story of one of today's most intriguing and inspiring stars—with information on...

➤ the near-nervous breakdown she suffered before turning her career around

➤ her long-distance romance with TV actor Dave Coulier, and how it came to an end

➤ her feelings about success and stardom

➤ how songwriter/producer Glen Ballard helped shape *Jagged Little Pill* and more

You Live, You Learn
THE ALANIS MORISSETTE STORY

D1571072

You Live, You Learn

THE ALANIS MORISSETTE STORY

Craig Tomashoff

BERKLEY BOULEVARD BOOKS, NEW YORK

YOU LIVE, YOU LEARN: THE ALANIS MORISSETTE STORY

A Berkley Boulevard Book / published by arrangement with
the author

PRINTING HISTORY
Berkley Boulevard edition / August 1998

The Penguin Putnam Inc. World Wide Web site address is
http://www.penguinputnam.com

ISBN: 0-425-16414-4

BERKLEY BOULEVARD
Berkley Boulevard Books are published by The Berkley Publishing Group,
a member of Penguin Putnam Inc.,
200 Madison Avenue, New York, New York 10016.
BERKLEY BOULEVARD and its logo are trademarks belonging to
Berkley Publishing Corporation.

PRINTED IN THE UNITED STATES OF AMERICA

10 9 8 7 6 5 4 3 2 1

ACKNOWLEDGMENTS

This project wouldn't be in your hands now if it wasn't for the hard work and kind words of many people. First, thanks to Miro Cernetig, Ann at Saban, Marcia Ricketts at NBC, Maria Kleinman, Bill Farley, and Mara Mikialian for their help in my research. Next, my appreciation goes out to James Muretich, Larry LeBlanc, Mayor Jacquelin Holzman and, most of all, Dominic D'Arcy, for letting me interview them whenever I had to. (And a second thanks to D'Arcy for his own terrific music.) Also, Michelle Steuven at *People* deserves special accolades for her diligent photography advice, as does Lynda Wright, who really knows how to wield a red pencil.

I'm also eternally grateful for the tolerance of Jack Kelley and Joe Treen at *People*, who allowed me the time to work on this project, and the efforts of my agent, Jane Dystel, who got this whole thing off the ground. Special nods go to Martha Bushko and Denise Silvestro at Berkley, for answering every one of my dumb questions, and to the moral support offered by Peter Ajemian, Kevin Coyne, David Millman, Mark and Lesley Holdom, and Tom Cunneff. I also want to thank all the fans—Dan the Alanis Man, Liza, Kathy, MCHoney, Robert, Jenn, Dawn, Will, and Tim—for showing their support of their favorite singer.

Finally, thanks to my parents, Walt and Barbara, and to my beautiful wife, Judy, and incredible son, Roman. You're the best inspiration a writer can have.

Introduction

*N*obody could have guessed things would turn out this way.

Nonetheless, it's December 14, 1996, in Honolulu, Hawaii, and there she is in all her multiplatinum glory. Alanis Morissette stands by Taylor Hawkin's drum kit, smashing at the skins to the point where one more blow will pummel them into a pile of dust, leading the crowd in a chant of "We will rock you!" Next, she's standing in front of the thousands of people who have jammed into Richardson Field on this gray, rainy afternoon, intently strumming the chords to her hit "Head over Feet" while one bare-chested guy after another gets body-passed in front of the stage. When she launches into "Hand in My Pocket" and comes to the line about using her out-of-pocket hand to flash a peace sign, the crowd responds almost as one, raising two fingers to flash the sign right back to her.

Her conquest of both the music world and popular culture will be complete in just a few minutes, when this final show of her juggernaut of a tour concludes. It will mark the end of the beginning of one of the most remarkable career turnabouts in rock history. At this very minute, however, the unassuming twenty-two-year-old in T-shirt, baggy cutoffs, and black tennis shoes, who is running across the stage flailing her long, dark hair as if it were a weapon, doesn't seem to care that she has more people hanging on her every word than most presidents do. She just looks happy to be here.

It's quite a contrast from just two years earlier. If anyone had suggested to you that by the end of 1996, a Canadian singer-songwriter and former pop princess unknown in America would become a best-selling singer here, you would have laughed off the idea. Who would possibly be foolish enough to put down money saying she'd end up releasing the most popular debut album ever by a female artist, embarking on a tour that would get her to twenty-eight countries for 252 shows in a year and a half, and earn a cool $22 million by the time she was twenty-three? Yeah, right. All that could happen. And the New Kids on the Block are about to go to the top of the charts again, too.

It's not like Cinderella stories don't happen in the music business. It's just that they usually don't have a happy ending. Artists can have their moment in the sun, but they are almost inevitably eclipsed by whatever the record label, and then the public, determine to be the Next Big Thing. And that was Alanis's tale. Sure, she'd experienced her fair share of success. Or, at the very least, she'd had enough of it to make her wary of it. Then, her star faded away.

Alanis had grown up a child prodigy, writing songs by the time she was nine, starring in a television show by the time she was ten, recording her first single by the time she was twelve. Hers was a childhood filled with ambition and achievement, something rare even in show-biz capitals like Los Angeles and New York, let alone her hometown of Ottawa, Canada. But Alanis hadn't stopped there. She didn't seem to know how.

She was singing professionally when she was fourteen, and had become Canada's reigning pop princess by the time her eighteenth birthday rolled around. Alanis Morissette was a marketing department's dream. An exceptionally bright and beautiful teen with big hair and small skirts, she could charm any audience with her innocently flirtatious lyrics and danceable tunes that were the musical equivalent of a Big Mac (they're all done the same way, no matter where you go, and that's the point). If America could have its Debbie "Electric Youth" Gibson, then by God, Canada was going to have its Alanis Morissette. And she was more than up for the task.

At first, she seemed perfectly cast to play the role of national sweetheart. She'd already auditioned for the part, playing an irresistably adorable young girl named Alanis on the television show *You Can't Do That on Television* before she was a teenager. Soon, she was performing in local talent contests and festivals in and around Ottawa, even flying off to Europe to make a music video to accompany a song that she had written, recorded, and released independently on a label she had started. Within a few years of that experience, she was not only entertaining heads of state at the Canadian prime minister's home (singing "O Canada"), but also holding court with them about political issues facing the country's music industry.

Naturally, when you're on this kind of a roll, things couldn't end there. The teen prodigy got a recording deal with a major label, and a 1991 self-titled disc with tunes that snapped and popped like bubble gum sold like crazy. She was voted Canada's Most Promising Female Artist at the Juno Awards, her country's version of the Grammys. Meanwhile, she started dating a television star nearly twice her age named Dave Coulier, and had entrée to the hottest nightspots in town. All this and she had yet to graduate from high school, where she was still managing to be a straight-A student. Life was picture-perfect. And she certainly seemed taken with all that was coming to her, gushing in a note published in the Ottawa *Sun* just before the Juno Awards, "It's Juno weekend and my dreams are coming true."

And then Cinderella left her slipper at the ball. Popular music tends to change like summer weather in the Midwest, with something new and different constantly blowing in to replace whatever had been heating things up five minutes earlier. So, when Alanis released a follow-up to her first

CD, which had come out only a year earlier, she was already yesterday's news. Nobody even noticed that with the second disc, her music and her words had grown up a bit. And why would they? She had officially become the Molly Ringwald of the music world, over-the-hill before she was old.

When you've made it to the top, no matter how briefly, you've also got a long way to fall. Alanis took a long tumble, first to Toronto, where she ran to escape her poofy-haired past. She kept up a positive attitude for those around her, constantly writing songs with dozens of local songwriters. But, although it may not have been readily apparent to those who knew her, something inside her had changed. There's nothing like having it all and quickly losing it to make you question what it is you were after in the first place. And why you were after it at all. Alanis often just sat alone some nights on a rock in Toronto's Beaches area, looking out at the water and contemplating the mess she figured her life had turned into. She'd spent so long following the textbook plan for becoming everyone's little darling, she seemed to have lost track of who she really was and what she really wanted to say.

Life didn't get much better when she fled even further away, to Los Angeles, where she was promptly mugged. All she had going for her was Glen Ballard, a singer/songwriter/producer who was nearly twice her age and going through an identity crisis of his own. Also a former musical prodigy, who wrote his first song at the age of six, Ballard had been essentially written off by critics as a pop lightweight because of his work with the likes of Michael Jackson and Wilson Phillips. They figured teaming him with Alanis and expecting a fiery, soul-baring collection of tunes was like throwing Celine Dion and Michael Bolton into the studio together and expecting them to come up with a searing alternative-rock hit. The odds were clearly against Alanis and Ballard, but management sensed the pair were capable of material much deeper than they'd been given credit for.

Even after Alanis and Ballard put together an album's

worth of material, with the tunes being written at the rate of one a day and then recorded in Ballard's home studio, expectations were decidedly low. Her own management company, which had encouraged the moves to Toronto and then Los Angeles in pursuit of her career revival, wasn't betting on more than a couple hundred thousand in sales for the CD, which had been titled *Jagged Little Pill*—as in the bitter one life forces you to swallow sometimes. Despite initial interest from a handful of record companies, no label was willing to take a chance on the disc except another underdog, Maverick Records, a company that had yet to be perceived as much more than a vanity project for its founder, Madonna.

So in June 1995, with virtually no fanfare, the CD was released. There were no massive advertising blitzes, no talk show bookings, no silly promotional giveaways to entice critics to listen. There was really only one promotional tool. The music. In particular, a song called "You Oughta Know." The first tune from *Jagged Little Pill* to get radio and video airplay, it was an instant success. The kind of song that makes you pull over to the side of the road when you first hear it, so you can soak it all in. You'd wait all night in the car just to find out who sings this bolt of lightning.

With rock hooks as sweet as the lyrics were angry, this bitter attack on an older ex-lover had everything going for it. Including the phrase, "Are you thinking of me when you fuck her?" and a fond memory of oral sex in a movie theater. This was the perfect way to get attention. It was titillating, nasty, controversial. All of which makes for a perfect novelty hit, with Alanis Morissette quickly being written off by some critics as the Girl Who Used the F Word or That Pissed-off Chick Singer. Within a few weeks of its release, however, something amazing began to happen. The song only got more popular, and album sales rapidly closed in on one million.

The success of *Jagged Little Pill* had at least a little something to do with the timing of its release. The rock scene was experiencing a small surge in powerful female artists—Melissa Etheridge, Sheryl Crow, Liz Phair. They had all received rave reviews and a fair amount of commercial success, but still, there seemed to be something missing. They were stuck in their own individual niches, unable to break into the mainstream and become a certified cultural event the way male rockers do. Until Alanis arrived, with the perfect combination of melody and meaning.

Her music had touched a national nerve. It literally leapt off the CD player and into your head, your heart, and your feet, all at the same time. It made you think, it made you feel, and it made you want to climb into the mosh pit, a very rare combination. In her songs, she sang of personal empowerment, of learning from your mistakes and using that knowledge to live life on your own terms. You live, you learn.

To the tens of thousands of teens and young adults around the United States, who were continually being written off by their elders as a generation of directionless slackers, Alanis's songs were like a life preserver. She understood what their lives were like. After all, she was one of them. Each tune was more like a diary entry, with Alanis candidly discussing her struggles with relationships, her career, her family and friends. She was purging all of the resentment and negativity that had accumulated in her psyche during those years she pretended to be the wholesome teen dream, and the world was ready to identify with her.

Naturally, not everyone bought into her dramatic story. She shied away from doing much publicity, particularly when it came to mentioning her pop past in Canada. To do so would mean dealing with the question that would linger over her career for months to come: How does one change her life and style so drastically? Keeping a low profile, playing only small clubs instead of the bigger arenas her record sales commanded, added to her mystique. She even turned down a lucrative spot on that summer's big Lollapalooza tour, trying to avoid becoming too big too soon. Some critics, particularly in her homeland, suspected the worst in these moves. This sort of micromanagement of a career certainly opened her up to accusations that she was little more than a slick marketing phenomenon. To the naysayers, she was just this year's model, cashing in on yet another trend.

And that cash was certainly rolling in. The occasional critical barbs were balanced by plenty of rave reviews of *Jagged Little Pill,* and sales continued to soar into the millions, past all the precious metals: gold, platinum, then double platinum. Cinderella had been given the glass slipper, yet she rejected it in favor of a pair of comfortable sneakers. The bigger she got, the more she tried to avoid the spotlight. This wasn't the way the game was supposed to be played, but there she was, winning anyway.

That explains the mischievous smile she is beaming to the throng in Honolulu. The long, strange trip that has been Alanis Morissette's life has finally come to this denouement. The tour is over. *Jagged Little Pill* is beginning to slide down the charts. There are no more awards left to win. Alanis has nothing left to prove. It's time to have some fun.

Her bandmates drape banners emblazoned with the words "For Sale" over their equipment. While they play "You Learn," she starts up a cream pie fight with the backstage crew. Then there's the Silly String attack, which leaves everyone on the stage covered with all sorts of muck, including Alanis herself, whose face and T-shirt are speckled with bits of white foam. So much for the poster child for female rage; Alanis looks like nothing more than a happy, successful young woman having a lot of fun.

Alanis and the band eventually exit stage right and head off to a tent, where she calls for "one last huddle" and offers up tight, personal hugs for each member of the group. You know those celebration scenes in the winning locker room after a World Series or Super Bowl? There is the same feeling in the air right now. A long season's worth of battles are over, and at least for this go-around, only the champions have been left standing.

Love her music or hate it, there's no denying that her ride to the top has been a remarkable one. It's like watching

Macaulay Culkin grow up to be Harrison Ford. Sure some canny marketing may have played a role in her transformation from dance diva to Voice of Her Generation, but you don't get this popular with just a gimmick. So how did Alanis persevere through her days as a child star if she truly didn't enjoy them? Why did she decide that her life had spun out of her control? How did she manage to rein it back in? What was the key to her success? At least one clue is still back out there on the stage. The place is littered with everything from food to flowers to clothing. This is the way the *audience* is supposed to leave the venue looking, not the band. But the thing of it is, the dividing line between Alanis and her audience has become a very thin one.

There's no denying that her life was not like those of her fans. This was a kid who spent her teen years playing at the Canadian prime minister's house and sipping tea in Paris with Bob Hope. Still, her music has found a way to cut through it all and connect with some very basic emotions.

"I never considered myself to be a very radical kind of person," she explained in one of her earliest interviews to promote *Jagged Little Pill*. "That's why the response is a little overwhelming. People are saying to me, 'You're saying things no one's ever said.' And I'm thinking, 'Am I really?' I'm not doing anything that isn't just human."

This is the thread that stitches together Alanis Morissette's life and her career. She's a woman who has long been on a search for herself, and by going on that journey, she ended up finding everyone else. It's not just her music that has inspired a generation. So, too, has the story of her struggle to make that music.

One

Deep down, the singer always knew. There was never any doubt about making it.

So what if growing up in Ottawa didn't offer the same opportunities as coming of age in one of the entertainment capitals south of the border, like New York or Los Angeles? If you've got the talent and the desire, there is nothing that can hold you back.

The singer was already performing professionally before becoming a teenager. Record company bigwigs then discovered this burgeoning talent. A debut single was cut by the age when most adolescents' biggest accomplishment is passing their driver's license test. And by the time most teens are graduating from high school, the singer had blown out of town in search of something bigger and better. Within a very brief period of time, the singer was writing tunes that topped the charts in both Canada and the United States.

"It's one of those things that's in your blood," the singer would say in an interview years later. "I always had the desire. I was like a junkie. From a very young age, this—to be a singer and songwriter—is all I wanted. Everyone thought I was crazy."

But Paul Anka wasn't nuts. He was merely one of a whole host of Ottawa natives during the past several decades to emerge from Canada's cozy capital city and make it big in the entertainment world. The late *Bonanza* star Lorne Greene, actor Dan Aykroyd, anchorman Peter Jennings, comic Rich Little, writer Margaret Atwood, rocker Bryan Adams, and folk-rock singer/songwriter Bruce Cockburn all grew up in this vibrant city of roughly 300,000 people, located 100 miles west of Montreal, a little more than 200 miles northeast of Toronto, and approximately 50 miles north of New York State.

Because Ottawa is the home to Canada's federal government, it would be only natural to think of it as a place teeming with professional bureaucrats, lobbyists, and the like. To some extent, it is a city that has an excessive interest in the practical, the here-and-now, the next election. As its litany of famous former residents indicates, however, Ottawa is also a lively, enriching town that offered them plenty of cultural advantages. From the National Gallery of Canada, which features the world's most comprehensive collection of Canadian artwork, to the annual Winterlude celebration of the arts, to the acclaimed Ottawa International Jazz Festival, this has long been a city that strives to be its nation's spiritual as well as political capital.

So, it's not nearly so surprising that this picturesque place could produce the most popular and beguiling female singer/songwriter of the late '90s. Ottawa was where it all began for Alanis Nadine Morissette, born on June 1, 1974, along with her twin brother, Wade. Her father, Alan, is a Canadian native who was a pretty fair athlete, playing fullback for the St. Patrick's College football team in the 1960s. He would grow up to be a schoolteacher and, eventually, principal of Ottawa's Our Lady of Fatima Elementary School. Not coincidentally, Alanis's mother, the former Georgia Feuerstein, was also a teacher. She had moved to Canada after escaping Hungary during the anti-Communist insurrection in 1956. The couple met while still quite young, in a scene that came right out of some achingly sweet, romantic ballad. Alan approached his future bride on

an Ottawa playground and said, "I'm gonna marry you."
He knew what he wanted. Then he went and got it. Not
unlike the daughter he and Georgia would eventually have.

"My parents are outgoing, worldly, direct people who
are very cute together," Alanis would later explain, also
describing them as "very free-spirited, curious people."
They had one child, a son, Chad, two years before Alanis
and Wade came along. During their first few years together,
the family moved on a fairly regular basis. Alan and Georgia had both taken jobs teaching the children of military
personnel, and eventually packed up the kids and headed
for a base in Lahr, West Germany. From the time she was
three until she was six, Alanis got to experience life abroad.
Okay, so perhaps being three years old and hanging out
with a bunch of Army brats isn't exactly exotic, especially
when your parents are not even in the military themselves.
Still, it also wasn't your typical childhood experience.

Not suprisingly, then, Alanis was not your typical child.
Having teachers for parents instilled the value of education
in her very early on, so by the time the Morissettes returned
to Ottawa, she was already demonstrating some amazing
brainpower, plenty of which was reflected in her early ap-
titude for music. Already (when Alanis was only four years
old), friends and family had detected her affection for singing. *Grease* was the worldwide smash hit at that time and,
like kids everywhere, she had rushed to see the film. For
days after going to hear Olivia Newton-John and John Tra-
volta belt out songs like "Summer Nights" and "You're
the One That I Want," she would wander around performing the tunes for anyone in the family who wanted to listen.
And probably some who didn't after a while.

"After I saw that [movie], it was, 'How could anyone
want to do anything else?' " she would explain several
years later.

All of this sounds like some sort of vintage Kodak moment, something so gosh-darn sweet and innocent that it
inspires everyone who sees and hears the child perform to
pinch her cheek and gush about how cute the kid is. Alanis,
however, wasn't performing these songs just to be every-

one's sweetie. Even her mom would later admit that her young daughter was certainly no "cutesie." This girl was serious about playing around with music.

She started noodling with the piano right about the time the Morissettes moved back to Ottawa, but that wasn't necessarily an unusual activity. Just ask any kid whose parents signed him or her up for piano lessons at an early age if for no other reason than the universal parental excuse— "It'll be good for you." Instead of being an instrument of torture, however, the piano was Alanis's release. By age seven, she also found another way to let the music flow through her, taking up dance as another hobby.

Within two years of that, she took her love of music and a gift for coming up with catchy melodies to the next level. She started tinkering around with writing her own songs. For most performers, it takes years to go through enough life experiences to have something to say in your music. What's a nine-year-old girl supposed to sing about? The heartbreak of getting cooties from the boys out on the playground? Once again, though, Alanis was no typical prepubescent girl. She worked on tunes like one called "Fate Stay with Me," a little ditty in which she told off an ex-boyfriend. Not entirely unlike the lyrical sentiments that would make her world-famous a decade later.

Both she and her twin brother, Wade, showed enough musical promise to stand out in their class at Our Lady of Fatima. And that's where she crossed paths with the first of several men who would help provide her with the opportunity to utilize her ambition and move on to the next level.

Dominic D'Arcy was well known to the city of Ottawa long before he and Alanis would ever meet. Born in 1939 in northwestern Quebec, he moved to Ottawa and joined the city's police force in 1965. Having grown up in a musical family, though, there was no way he could give up his love for singing songs and entertaining people. So, he quickly managed to find ten like-minded souls in the department and created a group he called the Ottawa Police Folk and Country Music Show.

That conglomeration didn't last very long, and within a few years, D'Arcy was performing his mix of Irish songs, pop tunes, and humor as a solo act. In 1975, he even recorded and released a single, "Come On, Listen." Meanwhile, he still tried to hold on to his job as a cop. "I chase bank robbers by saying, 'Stop or I'll sing,' " he loves to joke. Maintaining this musical career and playing in concerts "from Nashville to the North Pole" while still busting bad guys didn't sit well with his superiors.

"I used to be asked to resign often because of my music," he says. "When I was a young detective, I was told, 'Drop your guitar and we'll promote you.' I kept going, though. I worked hard as a cop, but I love my music. Anybody can have their dream, and I'm proof."

That's the message he had given to the youth of Ottawa for years, doing his show at school assemblies and working with youngsters he came across who happened to have a talent for singing or performing. He would eventually go on to develop the Dominic D'Arcy Talent Development Foundation, which uses private donations to assist the entertainment careers of the young children who qualify for the program. Alanis Morissette is without a doubt his greatest discovery.

"I was at the Holy Family Catholic School in Ottawa one day and noticed that at an assembly, a teacher had one of the classes sing 'My Canada,' " D'Arcy recalls. "I'm always on the lookout for talent, and I saw this young lady and her twin brother in the class. She had this great smile that I'll never forget. After the song, I went over to her and said, 'What's your name?' She just smiled at me and said, 'My name's Alanis.' "

At that point, Georgia, who had also been there listening to Alanis and Wade's class, popped up to speak to D'Arcy. Within a few minutes, he had an invite to the Morissettes' house for lunch.

There, he got to hear more music from the ten-year-old. She grabbed a TV remote control, pretending it was a microphone, and ran through a rendition of "Fate Stay with Me" in order to impress D'Arcy. The plan worked. He was so enthused by what he heard, they forged a partnership that would last for the next four years.

D'Arcy and his group of talented youngsters performed all around town, singing at nurseries, senior citizen homes, parks, on television shows. It didn't take long before Alanis was the star attraction at these shows. Wade, meanwhile, preferred to spend his time chasing his dream of becoming an Olympic swimmer. Despite Alanis's age, D'Arcy knew right from the beginning that there was something special about her.

When she would perform gigs at other schools, D'Arcy was fond of telling the kids who attended to get her autograph then because they'd wish they had it in a few years. And when young Alanis would meet with anyone who wanted to compliment her afterward on her performance, she would inevitably utilize one of D'Arcy's most important tips: Always look people in the eye and say thank you very much.

This is one lesson that perhaps never took as well as he thought it did. Years later, Alanis would recall how she would "say 'Thank you' for a compliment and think, 'You don't know how terrible I am!' It was a little bit of a drug for me. I wound up with all this adulation, and at that age you don't know what self-esteem is."

These insecurities were pretty well hidden back then, though. To those who worked with her, she came across as the sweetest, brightest, most talented kid in town.

"You'd try to speak to her as a ten-year-old, and she would look at you as if she was thinking, 'I knew that,' " D'Arcy says. "There was never a doubt that she could be what she wanted to be, whether it was a lawyer or singer or even prime minister."

So what is it that kept her so focused, so smart, at such a young age? She has said that she felt she had to prove herself. "I found something I could do that a lot of people wanted me to do. Anything to feel like a good girl. I was a smart kid at school, and excelling in show biz got thumbs-up across the board—from teachers to grandma—except for my schoolmates."

Those problems with her peers would apparently get worse in high school, as her fame grew to be nationwide. And that process really began when she landed a recurring role on a series called *You Can't Do That on Television*, a sort of preteen version of *Saturday Night Live*. The Canadian version of the program, which aired in that country from 1979 until 1995, was merged with an American version by the time Alanis joined the cast in 1984. (The show continued to be rerun on the Nickelodeon cable channel in the United States into the mid-1990s.)

D'Arcy remembers mentioning Alanis to a friend of his who worked on the show and "she jumped right in there," getting her first professional acting gig after beating out roughly three hundred other kids during an open casting call. It wasn't exactly Shakespeare in the Park. It wasn't even Shakespeare in the shopping mall. It was just meant to be a little harmless fun for its preteen audience, and acting wasn't necessarily required. Only enthusiasm, which Alanis had plenty of.

According to Geoffrey Darby, one of the show's directors at the time, the idea was to use real kids and have them essentially play themselves. They'd go to school all day, rehearse four evenings a week, and shoot the show on the weekends. The kids didn't necessarily want to use their experience on the series as a stepping-stone to stardom. Darby would tell them that this was "just a phase in your life. . . . After this, go back to your life and be normal." That certainly applied to Alanis, whom Darby never figured would pursue acting as a career. Likewise, he never anticipated her working as a singer at any point down the road because she "hid that talent under a barrel from us."

Her primary interest was just to spend her time on the set hanging around with the adults rather than with the other kids, according to Darby. Even at this time in her life, she just seemed to have more in common with people two and three times her age. She also stood out because she was the smart, pretty, and vivacious one in the group.

She didn't have to do much on the program. The primary goal of many skits was to see which cast member would end up with a truckload of icky green slime dumped on him or her. On several occasions, that lucky person turned out to be Alanis. Perhaps this wasn't the most enjoyable way to spend an evening, but she tried to be a good sport about the whole situation. "It was a good, stupid, sarcastic kind of show," she would later say of the experience.

A typical gag would go something like this: Alanis stands onstage with three fellow actors, looking painfully thin, her hair cut very short. There's something almost tomboyish about her appearance. In the skit, her new boyfriend is about to hit the road as a big-time rock star. "I just began liking you, but now you'll be away all year," she says with a pout.

The boy has the perfect solution. Why don't he and his friends form their own band, so they can be together all the time? The only question is, what should they name the group? One kid says, "Beats me." This is dismissed because Alanis's beau "doesn't like the sound of it." The next kid says, "I'm thinking, I'm thinking." That one won't do, the beau explains. It's too intellectual.

He turns to Alanis, looking for her suggestion. "I don't know," she says. And that's when the slime pours down on her head. The beau swears he had nothing to do with it. It's just that anytime anyone says, "I don't know," they get slimed. Alanis isn't convinced, turning away and telling him, "And now I will hate you."

And so it went, with her always playing the love interest to the two male leads. Because Alanis was so flirtatious and fun-loving when the cameras weren't rolling, the writers decided to transfer that persona to the show. She was the interest of the boys in real life, so why not let her be the romantic interest of the boys on the series? It was a move that didn't win her many young female fans. Alanis was only ten, but she'd already developed a complicated love life. She got hate mail from young girls who perceived her as a romantic rival, since she was constantly cast as the girlfriend of the show's attractive male leads. "It wasn't the best experience," she has recalled.

In the end, though, her days on *You Can't Do That on*

Television did provide her with a bit of a reward. Instead of squandering the money on clothes and toys, or dropping it into a college fund, she poured most of the cash she earned from her season on the program into recording a version of "Fate Stay with Me." On the flip side, she performed another of her own compositions, this one another tune of romantic yearning entitled "Find the Right Man." Along with a few local musicians she had gotten to know, including keyboardist Linsey Morgan and guitarist Rich Dodson, Alanis went into an Ottawa studio and cut her very first single before her eleventh birthday.

She was just a kid who should have been in way over her head. Most of her fellow musicians had been playing longer than she'd even been alive. Dodson and his old band, the Stampeders, had even had a Top 10 hit in 1971, "Sweet City Woman." Once again, though, she was determined not to act her age. It's no surprise that her music years later would offer empathy and advice to the lovelorn. She was already doling out the words of wisdom before she hit high school.

"I used to spend all kinds of time with people who were much older, so I was sitting in the producer's car, talking," Alanis has recalled. "I was actually giving him marriage advice, because he was in the middle of this divorce. I was going on and on about marriage and how it works. Then he looks at me, shakes his head, and goes, 'You're right—and that's what's blowing me away. . . .' "

With the help of Alan and Georgia, Alanis set up a record label of her own, Lamor Records. Two thousand copies of "Fate Stay with Me" were pressed up and released in the Ottawa area. The idea wasn't so much to make money off the single but to create something much more important. The Buzz. The forceful voice that bulldozed its way through the otherwise lightweight tune might get people talking about the talented young girl who continued to sing with D'Arcy at schools and parks around Ottawa. Who knows? Perhaps a real record company might even hear it.

Even though no major label deal suddenly surfaced, she continued to sing and catch the ear of more men in a po-

sition to help her. The next one up was a singer/songwriter
named Kenneth Gorman, who was also an English teacher
at Immaculata High, the middle school she was attending.
He was helping organize a talent show in the school auditorium one day when he heard the sultry sounds of a
young girl singing. Gorman whirled around to see the
twelve-year-old in a baggy sweatshirt, jeans rolled up to
her ankles, and a pair of white sneakers, barely moving
from the center of the stage as she sang.

Alanis suddenly hit a very high note that cut through the
air with such piercing precision that Gorman had to cover
his ears. That's why he felt compelled to speak to her after
she had finished, advising her that she could improve her
sound simply by moving the microphone away from her
mouth on strong notes and bringing it in closer when it was
time for the softer ones. She smiled the same smile that
had already captivated D'Arcy, thanked him, and went back
to work.

The two quickly became friends and ended up performing together a short time later, during the intermission of a
show by the school band. Once again, Alanis didn't hesitate
when it came to telling an older man what to do. They may
have been senior to her, but she was never one to be particularly deferential. As she and Gorman rehearsed the song
they would perform, a spiced-up version of Elvis Presley's
"Can't Help Falling in Love," Alanis would make up their
harmonies on the spot. Because their voices didn't mesh
that well, she suggested a difficult chord change Gorman
could do on his guitar.

"I was hesitant to try it onstage in front of the whole
school in case she couldn't find the B-flat note . . . but
Alanis had no such qualms. 'Let's give it a try,' she said,"
Gorman has stated. So, in front of seven hundred people,
with Alanis relaxed and smiling throughout the tune, she
made it through the chord switch flawlessly. "To this day,
I don't know how she found that note, but I remember
thinking to myself, 'This kid is good.' "

As poised and professional as she appeared to be in public, however, there was still something of the innocent child

left in her in private life. Once she showed up for singing practice, according to Gorman, chomping away on a piece of gum. He warned her that she couldn't sing and chew at the same time, so she offered a simple solution to the dilemma. She swallowed the gum.

" 'Don't swallow the gum!' I admonished her. 'It'll stay in your stomach for seven years,' " Gorman has recalled. " 'It will?' she responded, grimacing and holding her stomach."

Not long after that day, Alanis came to Gorman's classroom clutching an album and practically gushed, "Wanna buy my record? I've been selling them on the bus. Just sold one to the woman sitting beside me." This sort of brash behavior might be off-putting coming from some twelve-year-olds, but when it was Alanis, it came across as something kind of cute.

"Alanis did not consider her behavior eccentric. She saw herself as merely taking the first steps down a path that would eventually lead to superstardom as a singer-songwriter," Gorman has said. "Such an outcome was not a mere possibility or even a probability. In her mind, it was a certainty."

With an attitude like that, then, it wasn't surprising that she made another sale right then and there, and autographed her friend and mentor's copy with this: "Mr. Gorman, just think, you've taught me all I know, and I'll never swallow gum again."

It wasn't too long after that day that Alanis graduated from grade 8 and left Immaculata and Gorman behind to attend Ottawa's Glebe Collegiate School, where to nobody's surprise she would wind up enrolled in the special program for gifted children. True to the lyrics of her very first recording, however, fate continued to stick right by her side. She had managed to attract yet another believer in her abilities, another male mentor waiting to keep her career moving ever-upward.

This time, it was a former world-class figure skater who had retired from competition to produce local arts and entertainment festivals in Ottawa. Stephen Klovan had been hired to come up with the entertainment for a local arts and music showcase known as the Tulip Festival. He wanted to find kids who could perform in a combination fashion show/musical revue, and had nearly firmed up his cast when he got a phone call from a mother who said she had a daughter and her twin brother who might have something to offer. Naturally, she slipped in the fact that the girl had already had a year's worth of national television exposure.

Now this doesn't mean that Georgia was one of those pushy stage-mom types, the sort of mother who failed to live out her own artistic ambitions so her children must see the dream through for her. "I'm here to encourage her and support her, but not to push," she has said. And around the Morissette house, show business was never the number-one priority. Alan and Georgia tried to make sure their children led lives that were as centered and normal as possible.

"They would have meetings at the table when everyone was home to go over what had happened in their days, no matter who happened to be over there," says D'Arcy, who sat in on a few such confabs.

Klovan came over to the house, just as D'Arcy had a few years earlier, and left in awe of what he had just seen. He cast Alanis and Wade in the spring festival and they were instant hits. Dalmy's, a department store chain, was so impressed by the Morissette twins' performance that they were both signed up to travel around the Ontario-Quebec area promoting a new line of clothing stores called DalmysKids. Alanis even wrote a promotional jingle for the shops. Life-size pictures of her and her brother were placed in malls, and strangers who saw the real-life Morissettes would stop them to ask, "Aren't you the Dalmy's kids?"

This wasn't exactly the serious musical career Alanis was envisioning for herself. The gig had her modeling preppy, Gap-like sportswear and meeting and greeting strangers in malls. Far from being embarrassed by the situation, though, photos from this era reveal a happy teen who looks quite content with all that was coming to her. And Klovan was seeing to it that the offers didn't stop.

His next big break for his young protégée came in 1988.

The World Figure Skating Championships were to be held in Ottawa, and Klovan had been hired to work on a TV special about the big event. No sporting event can ever be complete without some version of that country's national anthem forcing the crowd onto its feet at the outset, and producers of the championships wanted a decent recording of "O Canada" to open up their grand spectacle. Klovan had a better idea. He convinced them to let Alanis, then thirteen years old, do the honors.

The producers agreed to the deal, and Klovan arranged to have a couple of local musicians back Alanis on the tune. They had to face facts, though. Sure national anthems are significant, emotional numbers, but they're not exactly the kind of song to light the fire of either an audience or the singers asked to perform them. It seemed only natural that if you're going to have a young spark plug of a singer do "O Canada," you better add some spice to it.

So, when Alanis stepped out in front of the crowd of ten thousand people, she launched into a well-rehearsed version of the national anthem that had a distinctive rock beat to it. The change was nothing radical. Nobody slam-danced to the tune or anything. Still, it was such a lively rendition that Alanis really got noticed in the days and weeks that followed. Eventually, she earned a reputation in Ottawa as "Miss O Canada," something that would come to haunt her throughout the rest of her time in her hometown.

She continued to sing at all sorts of local events, like football and baseball games, and her version of the national anthem was broadcast over the Glebe Collegiate intercom system most mornings. Alanis would sit in class and seem a bit shy about having to hear herself belt out the tune one more time, and some of her classmates would gently tease her about it. The buzz around town, though, was not quite so easy-going.

"As friendly and happy as she seemed when she was up there performing, there were people around town who would hear her and say, 'Oh, not her again,' " recalls a friend and Glebe classmate, Kathleen Clarkin.

These locals weren't the only ones getting a bit restless

with Alanis's burgeoning career. So was she. She had achieved some notoriety, but there was another level of achievement to get to. That's the trouble with ambition. It never lets you sit still and soak in the goals you've already attained. She was still only fourteen years old, but Alanis reportedly told her parents that it was time for her to move on to whatever the next phase of her career was to be. "Help me find another step," she told her parents.

Little did she know, she was already a good part of the way up the staircase leading her to success.

Two

*T*he story had taken on a familiar pattern. Whenever the young girl was starting to feel stretched to her creative limits, along came another adult into her life to help her along the way. They were drawn to her. Ask anyone who knew Alanis in her earliest days. She always seemed to be thirteen going on thirty thanks to a fierce combination of ambition and talent, and it was the grown-ups much more than her peers who appreciated that maturity.

She had one driving philosophy when she was younger: "I just looked around and tried to figure out what I wanted to do next. Some people had difficulty knowing how to treat me, but then others just treated me like an adult—and that was cool. Back then, it didn't seem unusual at all."

It also never struck her as strange that it was always men who were lending that helping hand. She wanted to be in the music business. For better or worse, men controlled that business. If she was ever going to make it, she had to listen to them—a harsh reality that would set the stage for plenty of the rage that went into *Jagged Little Pill* years later. There was, however, one woman from whom Alanis did seek help early in her career.

One day after mass, when she was still only twelve, she

got up the nerve to approach a fellow parishioner who happened to be part of a popular singing duo known as One-2-One. Louise (Sal) Reny, along with her songwriter/guitarist partner, Leslie Howe, had just released her group's debut album and it was moving up the charts when this young kid boldly stepped right up to ask for help in developing her music.

This sort of behavior from an adult might have come across as pushy, but when it's an enthusiastic preteen girl, it is gutsy and irresistible. Reny ended up going back to the same dining room table that D'Arcy and Klovan had also become familiar with. They had walked away with the clear impression that it was Alanis and not her parents who wanted her to achieve her dream of a recording career. Not so with Reny, however.

D'Arcy swears he never saw her folks force her into anything she didn't want to do during those dinner-table meetings, but Reny sensed something else. Georgia took control of the brunch the day of her visit, doing the bulk of the talking and leaving Reny with the clear impression that mom and dad were pushing for Alanis's success as much as Alanis was.

Even if some thought her parents were instrumental in Alanis's career, she didn't see anything unusual about the situation. She loved her family dearly, and the difficulties in their relationship didn't seem that much different from those experienced by any other daughter in any other family. "I just wanted to do whatever it took to get approval of my parents and the people I was working with at the time," she explained years later.

She didn't get a thumb's-up from Reny. At least not at that meeting. Like those who would come before and after her, she was quite taken by the way Alanis seemed "ten years older than anyone I knew, maturity-wise." She was also impressed with her vocal skills, and the fact that she had written several of her own songs. Still, this wasn't enough for her to start working with Alanis. Reny herself had missed out on plenty of growing up in high school because she was busy playing in a band, and couldn't recommend that life to someone else.

"I just thought she was too young, not that she wasn't good enough. I just thought, 'You should be having fun,'" she has explained.

They parted company, and Alanis continued her apprenticeship with Klovan. He had come up with another grand plan for her. She was as well known as she could get in and around Ottawa, and she'd already been on national television, so now it was time to go international. He got her a shot on the syndicated talent show, *Star Search,* in the fall of 1989. The program was a good launching pad if you wanted to shoot for the stars, giving the careers of future famous folks like Rosie O'Donnell and Sinbad a big boost. At roughly the same time, Georgia and Alan had a chance meeting in an Ottawa restaurant with Reny's partner, Howe. They had already met, when Howe was hired as one of the collaborators who helped create Alanis's version of "O Canada." As had become her custom, Georgia began talking to him about her daughter's musical talents and passed on a tape of some of her songs.

The timing was coincidental, but quite convenient. Howe and Reny were between One-2-One albums and looking for some work to do to tide them over. Perhaps shaping this young singer and her music into something marketable would do the trick. Her songs didn't light much of a fire for him, but there was a spark about the girl that intrigued him. What she lacked in songwriting ability she more than made up for in personality. He couldn't resist the confidence she displayed, and they went to work together right away.

Their initial goal was to come up with something innovative Alanis could use to wow the judges during her *Star Search* performance. Instead of working on an original number, they reworked the old Osmonds tune, "One Bad Apple." Howe helped pump up the lightweight ditty with his skill on the keyboards, and Alanis took his backing track with her to New York, where she was defeated in the first round of the vocalist category.

Winning or losing was, ultimately, irrelevant anyway.

What counted was the partnership with Howe. He and Reny had set up a studio in the basement of their townhouse on the east side of Ottawa, and Alanis would ride her bike there across town every day during her first year at Glebe Collegiate. The sessions would sometimes last well past dinnertime, and there were occasions when she would be writing and recording until one A.M.

It was slow going, taking Alanis's raw talent for singing and finding a sound that would be appropriate. And financially rewarding. One of the perky, exceedingly commercial pop numbers Howe, Reny, and fellow Ottawa musician Frank Levin had written for her was something called "Walk Away," in which a ticked-off Alanis is ready to take a hike rather than stick with a seemingly disinterested boyfriend.

They could have put the tune on a demo tape, along with a few others, and shipped it to record labels. To do so, however, would have meant tapping into only one aspect of Alanis's ability. As good as her singing was, it was her charming persona, her upbeat attitude, her ever-present smile that really sold her.

Then again, they might have had her perform a few showcase concerts in local clubs. This would have been tough to do, though, because the music Howe had recorded with her was heavy on computer-programmed synthesizers, precisely the sort of sound that is hard to re-create live.

So, instead of taking the normal route, Klovan and Howe came up with a plan to show off their young charge at her best. Why not produce a music video for "Walk Away"? And not only that. Why not make this clip look as exotic as the young girl singing the song? So it was decided. They'd take her to Paris, where she could bop around recognizable landmarks like the Eiffel Tower. The cost would no doubt be prohibitive, but you can't make money if you don't spend money. They went for it.

Klovan did see to it that they spent as little as possible. He was able to work out deals with an airline and Hilton Hotels. They provided plane tickets and hotel rooms in exchange for exposure in the video. Some Ottawans who knew and believed in Alanis's work also chipped in what they could, and soon she was off with Klovan, Howe, and local director Dennis Beauchamp for a ten-day jaunt around Paris to make the tape.

Conspicuous by their absence on this trip were Alan and Georgia. They had always been there before for their daughter, but this time, they decided to trust their instincts and let their fourteen-year-old girl go to Europe in the company of her mentors. After all, this wasn't some kid whose biggest thrill up until then was an overnight camping trip with the rest of her Brownie troop. Alanis already had more experience than many performers twice her age, with national television exposure and a record on her resume.

"When I was ten, I just started going around with people, doing different stuff: videos, acting, whatever," Alanis has said. "My parents let me go, they trusted the people [I was working and traveling with], and I wanted to be in the entertainment business. . . . I don't think any of us really thought twice about it."

To those unfamiliar with the people involved, it might have looked a little, well, compromising. A young girl was traveling to Europe with a group of older men, all of whom were somehow involved in the music industry. However, thanks to an upbringing that relied heavily on Catholic guilt, any sort of sexual misbehavior was totally out of the question. That applied whether she was hanging out in Paris or at home in Ottawa. On the plus side, this left plenty of time to concentrate on building her career. On the down side, though, it repressed a side of her that would only find expression when it came time to write *Jagged Little Pill*.

"My family went to church every Sunday," Alanis once told an interviewer. "My parents were pretty liberal, but while my brothers were allowed to have fun with their sexuality, I was this virgin that was held up on a pedestal."

She had to be the good girl, the one who made everyone oh so proud of her because she didn't succumb to temptation. Instead, she worked harder to make something of herself. Which she certainly did during that Parisian trip. It was the middle of the school year, but this kind of career opportunity doesn't happen very often, so she was allowed by her family to miss her classes and go overseas.

For more than a week, she and her fellow travelers worked on the video. They shot Alanis dancing happily on a Paris sidewalk. They caught Alanis spinning around by the Seine wearing a pretty floral print dress. They had her splash around, beaming that trademark smile, in a fountain near the Eiffel Tower. Even when they finished filming for the day, the work didn't stop. It would be time to hit the Paris nightclub scene, having wangled invitations like one to a party with Diana Ross and another to a cocktail reception for Bob Hope.

By the time they all got back to Ottawa, there was little doubt they had made the right decision. The video was quickly edited together, and a copy just happened to be sitting in Howe's basement studio on the day he met with John Alexander, who was director of Artists and Repertoire at MCA Records Canada and at MCA Canada Publishing. It was Alexander's job to locate and sign new artists for his company, getting both song recording and songwriting deals in place, and he wanted to see if Howe had something to offer.

Alexander knew what it was like to be a young musical sensation from Ottawa. He had been the lead singer for a band called Octavian, one of the city's previous success stories, during the mid-1970s. He got into music management in the early 1980s and in 1984 signed on at his MCA job. He'd never intended to stay there for very long. The idea was simply to gain some knowledge and some connections, then reenter the world of music management. Instead, he ended up working with Canadian artists like Allanah Myles, Rik Emmett, Sarah McLachlan, and Blue Rodeo.

Then, along came that fateful meeting with Howe. Alexander had been checking out the possibility of signing Howe and Reny to MCA and, after listening politely to some of their One-2-One material, was getting ready to go.

"Oh, by the way, I just did this. You want to listen to it?' '' Howe reportedly told the record company executive as he pulled out a copy of Alanis's video for "Walk Away." Alexander agreed to stick around, and couldn't resist what he saw up there on the television screen. There was a very professional Alanis bopping around to a very slick pop song on the very beautiful streets of Paris.

This wasn't necessarily good news to Reny. She was a bit aghast that her partner had decided to play the tape for a guy with whom *they* wanted to sign a deal. When she saw the interest creeping across Alexander's face, she knew that he was already thinking about how to make the still-fourteen-year-old Alanis the next big superstar from Ottawa.

Shortly thereafter, Alexander carted a copy of the video into the Toronto office of his boss, MCA Records Canada president Ross Reynolds. Reynolds popped it into his player and was also immediately struck by what he saw. It wasn't so much the music, which was catchy but not particularly ground-breaking, but rather the personality of this young girl that made him lean forward in his chair and take notice.

"She appealed to me somehow," Reynolds recalls. "She had that very hard-to-define star quality. There was this enormous self-confidence. You knew that in some way, she was going to be a star."

Alexander went back to Ottawa to have dinner with Alanis, at which point he told her that "I don't know how long it'll take or what it'll take, but I want to sign you." He was true to his word. Shortly after that meeting, Alanis inked a songwriting deal with MCA Publishing and got to work at Howe's studio on a debut disc for MCA Records Canada to consider releasing.

Working again with Howe and a local keyboardist/songwriter, Serge Cote, the now-fifteen-year-old girl got busy trying to come up with enough material to fill her first album, and keep up her grades and her friendships at Glebe Collegiate, a task that was already tough and would only get more so. No matter how much pressure she was under, Cote says, she always seemed to have everything under control and her tremendous vocal talents never faltered.

"The power and attitude of her voice always amazed me. It all just seemed to come so easily to her," he recalls. "She'd come into the studio, spend about ten minutes singing a particular track and say, 'Okay, I've got to get back to school now.' She was always so cheery about everything."

There was plenty to be happy about. MCA was supportive throughout the process, pushing Howe and Alanis to get their record done as quickly as possible. To make the young singer feel like part of the family, Reynolds even threw a party in his backyard to celebrate her birthday. That sort of thing doesn't happen much even for artists with twice her experience, but the label seemed to be quite confident that its investment in Alanis would pay off big-time. Her gregarious personality was too much to resist for anyone at the company who met the young girl.

"She bounced into the office one day with this big smile on her face," recalls Cameron Carpenter, who at the time worked with Alexander in MCA's A&R department. "She had tons of charisma, and seemed eager to learn."

However, back in the studio, all wasn't going particularly smoothly, at least at first. Howe had sunk a lot of his money and time into making an Alanis disc, and there was pressure to get it done and over to MCA as quickly as they could, according to Cote. They had put in a lot of effort trying to duplicate the happy-skippy feel of "Walk Away," but halfway through the writing process, something happened. They'd found a sound that seemed perfect for this teenage talent.

"There was this pivotal point where her style changed," recalls Cote, who now runs his own audio postproduction company, and continues to write and produce music in Ottawa. "The interest at first was in making songs like 'Walk Away,' which was kind of pop-rockish, but then we started experimenting, even though we didn't have a lot of time, and came across this sort of dance, drum-loopy kind of stuff. Everybody said, 'Do more like this.' "

The final tracks for the CD were laid down at Howe's studio between September and December 1990, and on April 23, 1991, MCA unleashed the ten-song disc on the Canadian public. Simply titled *Alanis*, it featured a black-

and-white shot of its namesake on the cover, pouting sexily for the camera. On the back, there was another black-and-white picture, with an unsmiling Alanis trying to look her toughest in a leather jacket, lounging against what looks like an alley wall.

This attitude, and the CD's music, fit in perfectly with much of what was popular at the time. New Kids on the Block, Debbie Gibson, and Vanilla Ice were all cranking out hits to party by, with catchy if impersonal synthesizer dance beats. The sound was all about teens getting teen feet moving. Revealing deep thoughts or working in complicated melodies was out of the question. Not that this was Alanis's fault, or some cynical marketing strategy designed to take advantage of a trend. She was simply taking the kind of music she knew, the sort of sound that her peers couldn't seem to get enough of, and giving it back with as much ability as she had.

One of Alanis's idols at the time was Janet Jackson, and the music on *Alanis* certainly reflects that adoration. Nearly every tune thumps in with the sound of drum machines, and tries to make up in energy what it lacks in real emotion. None of this was necessarily a bad thing. This was the sound that was in at the time. If you happened to hear any of the songs in the car on the way to school or work, it would be hard to resist pounding the dashboard in time to the beat. There's never been anything wrong with a good dance riff. It's just that in the case of Alanis's music, there was not much there to distinguish it from any other dance riff.

The lyrics are equally bland. The songs on *Alanis* have titles like "Feel Your Love," "Too Hot," and "Party Boy," and most feature such lyrical twists as "Give it to me like I'd like to give it to you" and "You gotta go for gold." On "Oh Yeah," Alanis even manages to rap a little, proudly announcing that just because she's sixteen doesn't mean she's a disco queen.

There were signs that she was trying to do something a bit more grown-up. Nothing on the level of *Jagged Little Pill*, certainly, but at least an indication that she was determined to be taken as an artist with serious potential. On the song "Plastic," she does attempt to make a statement about the materialism of the world by chastising those who use "a plastic card," as in Visa or Discover, to buy their dreams. And with "On My Own," she seems to be striking back at anyone who figured she was too young to be doing what she was doing, singing about a starry-eyed girl and those around her who think "they've got her all figured out."

Still, this wasn't exactly the sort of disc to make many critics' Top 10 lists. In fact, it wasn't the sort of disc that inspired many critical reviews at all. Yet, despite that lack of attention, "Too Hot" was picked as a single and sent out to radio and before long, it hit number four on the charts. On the strength of that song, the album also started selling. After three months, it had sold 30,000 copies. By the time the disc was finished, it would sell more than 100,000 copies, relatively small by U.S. standards but massive in Canada's smaller market. Alanis was a certified celebrity in her homeland.

Life had completely changed, and there was no going back. She was in demand everywhere she went, signing autographs and greeting well-wishers. This was precisely where she figured she was supposed to be.

"I've wanted this for so long. I imagined what it would be like and every time somebody comes up to me on the street or recognizes me in a restaurant, it's like . . . wow! I love it!" she gushed to one interviewer not long after *Alanis* was released.

By all outward indications, she was indeed having a great time living the life of a big-time recording artist. There were plenty of perks. MCA made sure she went to all the important record stores and radio stations around Canada to promote the album. She performed live a few times as well, once opening a concert for the already-melting Vanilla Ice. Singing at sporting events also became a specialty, with Alanis putting on a big halftime concert during a Canadian Football League game in Ottawa and later entertaining the crowd at a National Hockey League awards show by singing "Too Hot" in a referee's jersey while surrounded by dancers wearing rollerblades.

When it came time to do a video for one of the singles, she took charge of picking out the actors and actresses who would perform with her (one of whom was a young model named Matt LeBlanc, who would go on to fame and fortune of his own a couple of years later, costarring in the TV series "Friends"). When she showed up for an appearance at her hometown's Carlingwood Mall, twenty-five hundred fans mobbed the place to get a look at their local hero. Strangers were coming to the front door of the Morissette home in search of an autograph. The younger kids who were just entering her school would walk the halls in search of the new young superstar they now shared a building with, asking, "Where's Alanis?"

Even the Canadian Recording Industry Association (CRIA), the powerful organization that represents the political interests of the Canadian music business, took notice of this young Ottawa girl. Her hometown was, after all, her nation's capital, so anything she did there automatically received more attention. She had even spent her early teen years playing at the home of Canada's prime minister at the time, Brian Mulroney, after befriending his daughter.

When *Alanis* came out, she got to spend even more time at the residence, this time in a more official capacity. During the early 1990s, CRIA was lobbying for changes in the country's copyright act, and would often state its case at formal dinners with the prime minister. Alanis was occasionally brought in to sing the national anthem—by now her specialty—and then spend time chatting up the politicians from Canada and abroad about the need for copyright reform.

"There was no concern about her getting up in front of the prime minister or any visiting dignitary," recalls Brian Robertson, current president of CRIA. "She had the ability to recognize exactly why she was there. We'd brief her on the issues and then she'd get up and give a very accurate synopsis of what we wanted. She really helped our cause, laying the groundwork for what we had to talk about. It was more like dealing with an adult than with a young teen."

Though rock critics can normally be a pretty grumpy

group, many of them seemed somewhat taken with Alanis. Maybe they weren't that impressed with her music, but once they met her, it was another story altogether. After interviewing her, writers would sometimes gush about the sophistication and poise Alanis, now a seventeen-year-old, exhibited. She welcomed criticism about her music ("It's good for me," she told one critic), and never once doubted that she would be around for a long, long time.

"If you just stay yourself and keep coming up with good stuff, I don't see any reason why you'd die out," she explained to a reporter. "Trouble happens when people run dry and their second album isn't any good. That's when people turn to excuses like, 'Oh, she was only sixteen or seventeen or whatever.' "

There was just one small problem with all of this. Alanis really *was* only seventeen, and no matter how mature a teenager is, it's still awfully early to be experiencing the adrenaline rush of fame. Just ask Macaulay Culkin or the cast of the old TV series *Diff'rent Strokes*. Despite all the good things that were continually happening to her, Alanis would occasionally let down her guard enough to indicate this wasn't nearly as much fun as it might seem.

When she was doing her appearances at record stores, for instance, she often came across to those who saw her as quiet and timid. "She seemed new to the whole process," remembers an employee at one Ottawa CD shop. The Canadian correspondent for *Billboard* magazine, Larry LeBlanc, recalls meeting Alanis at the opening of a big store in Toronto and finding her to be "very shy. She seemed like somebody's prom date, standing there with people making a big fuss over her."

And, even though she had helped select them, she expressed some embarrassment over the hormone-heavy video for "Too Hot," which featured her cavorting with a group of beefcake guys. It was no doubt her Catholic upbringing talking when she said that "having a little sex thrown in there is okay . . . but there's no way I want people seeing me and saying, 'She's only sixteen? Oh, that little slut, what is she doing?' "

Despite her confidence in her ability to make music, and all the fancy trappings of fame that were coming her way, there was a fair amount of insecurity just waiting for the chance to consume her and all that she had worked so hard for. Alanis just didn't seem to want to admit that there was something wrong.

"Back then, I was a lot more worried about people's perceptions of me. I wanted their approval," she explained shortly after *Jagged Little Pill* was released and began exorcising some of these early demons. "I wanted their approval, so I always came across happy. I repressed a lot of stuff."

It may have been her love life that suffered the most. The songs on her first album certainly made her sound like a girl of the world, someone with the same sort of take-charge attitude toward men exhibited by singers like her favorite, Janet Jackson, and her future boss, Madonna. Still, Alanis had been so busy focusing on her career, she hadn't developed many romantic attachments.

Although telling a writer that she had "dated, like, a bazillion people," she would also admit that her songs didn't often have much to do with what went on in her real life. "I'm only seventeen and, as far as relationships, I haven't had any yet. I was just writing what I thought it would be like."

Her continuing success, as well as the fact that she spent much of her time hanging around adults rather than fellow teenagers, didn't make dating any easier. Even so, she didn't seem to want to change things. As 1991 came to an end and *Alanis* continued to sell well, her thoughts seemed to be focused on what she would be doing next with her music, not her social life.

The former couldn't have been better. She was already anticipating broadening her career into the United States. ("A lot of people say I'll be thrown to the wolves. . . . But I'm not really scared. I'm looking forward to it," she explained.) And there was the second album to start thinking about. The success of the first had put the pressure on her. She'd worked all of her young life to get to this place. There was no way she'd let herself slip and fall off the top of the charts now. She'd show the world she was no one-hit wonder.

She knew the basic gripe about her music. It was too fluffy. Easily replaceable by the next cute teen act that bopped onto the scene. The second disc, she would tell interviewers, had to "have maybe a bit more of a harder edge. It's not going to be as dance [-oriented]. But I say that now and if you put me in the studio tomorrow, I might write something completely different."

While talking confidently about her singing career, though, she would sometimes hedge her bets a bit, pondering attending college and studying psychology. Maybe she'd even follow in her parents' footsteps and get into teaching. These were nice thoughts, but not particularly realistic ones. Alanis's drive to be a singing superstar left no room for these less-glamorous pursuits.

She told interviewers she'd be in the music business "even if I wasn't a singer." The fact was, there really wasn't anything else she had prepared herself to do. "If I wasn't doing music, I wouldn't have any idea what I wanted to do."

Such comments at first sounded rather impressive. Here's a kid who knows what she wants, and she's not afraid to get it. Who knew what she might be capable of? At the same time, though, a statement like this was a clue to anyone willing to pay attention that something was wrong with her idyllic life. Her music was all about being young and having fun, but sometimes it seemed like she preferred to sing about those experiences rather than have them.

A teenager goes through enough pressures anyway, thanks to everything from dating to learning to drive, without also having to worry about how to please tens of thousands of adoring fans waiting for you to prove your success was no fluke. It's not like Alanis wasn't happy and grateful for all that she'd achieved, but whether she even realized it or not, hitting the big payday could cost her a personal life.

Three

Alanis had already done plenty of traveling in her young life, from her family's jaunt to Germany when she was three to the sojourn to Paris to make her first music video. Perhaps the most exciting trip she'd taken in her first seventeen years, though, was the trek from Ottawa down to Toronto in March 1992. This time, she wasn't traveling as a singer trying to make it. Now, she was a rising star.

She had gone for the Juno Awards, Canada's version of the Grammys. The success of her debut record, *Alanis*, had landed her three nominations—Single of the Year, Best Dance Recording, and Most Promising Female Vocalist. By this time, her CD had sold more than 100,000 copies in her native land, and a gushing Alanis could barely contain her excitement when she dashed off a postcard to her fans, which was published in her hometown paper, the Ottawa *Sun*.

"Talk about nerves! It's Juno weekend and all my dreams are coming true," she wrote. "After all the work, there's a chance I might just be rewarded with a Juno tonight. We won't talk about that, we don't want to jinx things, do we?"

Alanis went on, eagerly describing all the interviews she

had been doing with writers and disc jockeys from across the country, a task that was by now not very new but still apparently rather exciting for her. In between these chats, she kept on the go by attending seminars about the music business, putting in an appearance on MuchMusic, Canada's version of MTV, and rolling a few frames at the celebrity-filled Rock 'n Bowl tournament in nearby Scarborough.

She was enjoying it all, from the meet-the-nominees reception where she was greeted as the Next Big Thing by her new peers, to the intense rehearsals she went through to make sure her appearance on the show was just right. It wouldn't be until years after the Juno hoopla was nothing but a faded newspaper clipping that she would admit to herself and the world how unrewarding the whole situation really was.

"When I was younger, I always used to think that if you were to have a number-one record and win a Grammy award, your life would be wonderful . . . and everyone would love you. But the opposite is true," she would tell an interviewer.

Still, for this one weekend in Toronto, she was soaking up every ray of the spotlight. Her postcard even bragged of her "special Juno outfit": "I know for a fact that no other girl will be wearing it, because I helped design this with a friend—so I think I'm safe from copycats. . . . I'll be nervous all afternoon."

She needn't have worried. By the time the evening was over, she had won the Most Promising Female Artist award. Never mind that she didn't win in the other two categories she had been nominated for. She had proof that it wasn't just the kids buying her CD who understood what she was all about. Her peers had also recognized all the talents she'd been honing for nearly a decade.

"The amount of time I spent waiting in anticipation of what was going to happen was just insane," she explained that night. "Since I was nine years old, I wanted what I have now."

She may have finally gotten what she'd wanted, but back

home in Ottawa, it was becoming rather apparent that she had lost something along the way as well. Nowhere was that more evident than at Glebe Collegiate. Alanis made an effort to live as normal a life as possible, continuing her studies and trying to keep up her good grades despite the frequent promotional trips out of town to record and then promote her first CD. However, music always won whenever it went head-to-head with school.

"She was a good student and didn't fool around in class, but she could have done better except that her focus really seemed to be on her career," says Bruce MacGregor, her grade 9 English teacher and a fellow musician who still plays in a band with other Glebe instructors. "She was always taking chunks of time out to do music. Mentally, her primary goal was to be a music star, but she never really talked about that. She wouldn't walk around asking, 'Did you hear my record?' "

Flaunting her success just wasn't her way. Even during a grade 11 assembly, when she and brother Wade performed a song from *Grease*, she went out of her way to avoid being considered too showy by lip-synching to Olivia Newton-John instead of singing the tune. In fact, it seemed to some that she was downright shy about her remarkable abilities and accomplishments. MacGregor still treasures his memory of a day in 1991 when his band played at a local volleyball tournament, and Alanis and some friends showed up to watch the show.

"I introduced her as our up-and-coming star, and while everyone was looking around, going, 'Which one is she?' she looked really embarrassed," he explains.

When she was away from the studio and on her own, she certainly seemed like your average, fun-loving teenage girl. She hung out with friends, talking about boys, although "she always tried to switch the focus to others instead of herself" in such discussions, recalls her friend Kathleen Clarkin.

She was much better at giving romantic advice than she was at listening to it. Fellow musician and songwriter Cote remembers how he would talk to her about proper dating behavior, and "she liked to say what I should do on a first date. I like to talk, so she would tell me not to take a woman to a club first but rather a bar or restaurant, where we could speak to each other." When it came to talk about her love life, though, it was "boys this and boys that," Cote says, but never much detail.

When she had the time, she would lead aerobics classes at Glebe. And quite often, she could be spotted cruising around town in her Volkswagen Rabbit, which she had painted red to look more like the flashy car driven by one of D'Arcy's sons.

"I'd put pretend tickets on her car when she parked it at school, and all the kids would go around saying, 'Alanis got a ticket! Alanis got a ticket!' " D'Arcy recalls.

This mocking reaction was done in jest, but there was a serious undercurrent of resentment running through the Glebe hallways. Her success didn't endear her to many of her classmates, and they would let it slip out in very covert ways. She would hear the whispers—"There she is! There she is!"—as she walked to class, but acted as if none of this was a problem. Being a part-time high school senior/ part-time teen idol didn't faze her because, as she put it, "I love having a fast-paced sort of life, and there hasn't really been much trouble combining the two lives."

Alanis tried to put a good face on the situation, but those who were close to her could sense that all was not well.

"I know she went through a lot," continues D'Arcy. "She got the cold shoulder [at school]. It was jealousy in its purest form. She'd be on TV and winning a Juno award, then back in school and part of the gang. I do think she learned not to brag about her success, and not to say, 'Look what I did this weekend.' . . . But she went through hell with her peers."

Alanis was the perfect child, who had always been good at everything she did, from music to homework. By the time she finished her education at Glebe in the summer of 1992, she was rated an Ontario Scholar, meaning her grade-point average was 80 percent or above. She didn't smoke or drink. In short, she was the sort of kid only a parent could love, but other teens would wonder about. It's hard for them to really trust somebody their own age who doesn't *seem* like she is their own age. The truth was, she didn't always feel that she was somebody in charge of her own life.

Occasionally, others could tell something wasn't quite right. When Alanis sensed that classmates might be criticizing her behind her back, says Clarkin, "she'd sometimes joke about it and relax, like nothing bothered her, but you can only be polite to those who are rude to you for so long before you have to break down."

And that's apparently just what happened. In an interview years later, she would admit that she "freaked out" one day in her parents' house. They were busily preparing to head out of town for a business trip, and their daughter was slammed upside the head with the realization that maybe she had come too far too fast. She was almost through her childhood years, but had never really slowed down to enjoy them. Instead, her life seemed to have become about getting to the next accomplishment, the next level of glory.

"I'd taken too much on myself and for once, I dropped my facade of total assurance," Alanis would later explain. Obviously mortified by this sudden change in their daughter's demeanor, Alan and Georgia canceled the trip and stayed home to counsel Alanis in her hour of need. Whatever they said must have worked, because she threw herself right back to her grueling schedule. It would be a few more years before she would truly be able to identify and then cope with the stress that had been building up since the world took notice of her talent.

"There was an element of me not being who I really was at the time," Alanis has said. "It was because I wasn't prepared to open up that way. The focus for me then was entertaining people as opposed to sharing any revelations I had. . . . I had them, but I wasn't prepared to share."

Instead of forcing the issue, she did what she had always done—hang around with an older crowd of people. Who needs to talk about pep rallies and prom dates when you've

been at a dinner with the prime minister discussing business
policies? This wasn't arrogance or disrespect for her
schoolmates. There was a part of her that longed for a close
friend, a boyfriend, anybody closer to her own age that she
could connect with. It was just that Alanis had long seemed
like someone impatient with her own youth, eager to let
the adults know she was as talented and smart as any of
them. That meant she had little in common to talk over
with fellow seventeen-year-olds.

That's why it shouldn't have been as big a surprise as it
was that her first beau of any significance was an older man.
He was actor and comedian Dave Coulier, who at the time
was starring in two different shows on ABC, *Full House*
and *America's Funniest People,* when he met Alanis in
Montreal at the 1992 National Hockey League all-star
game.

She was there to sing her country's national anthem, and
Coulier had traveled out from Los Angeles to play in a
celebrity exhibition game prior to the main matchup. While
he stood on the blue line of the Montreal Forum, listening
to her sing, Coulier was startled to feel the elbow of legendary hockey star Gordie Howe poking him in the ribs.

"Did you see that? She looked right at you," Howe said
with a smile. By the time Coulier glanced back at her, however, Alanis was back into her song and paying no attention
to him.

They didn't connect on the ice, but later that evening, in
the lobby of the hotel they both happened to be staying at,
Coulier introduced himself to the young singer. Despite
their fourteen-year age difference, the couple hit it off. Like
every other grown-up Alanis encountered, he was immediately struck by how mature she seemed. Chronologically,
she may have seemed a bit young for him but mentally and
emotionally, she was his age if not older.

"She was one of the sweetest and brightest people I'd
ever met," Coulier has said. "And she had this great sense
of humor. You could say anything in front of her and she'd
go off with it."

For the next year, they would see each other whenever

they could. Which, unfortunately for them, was not very often. The Detroit native Coulier lived in Los Angeles, caring for his son from a previous marriage, while Alanis was still in Ottawa. The distance put a real strain on the relationship, but for a time, they made the best of it. Even though their time together was often very short, with Alanis heading off to work on her songwriting or Coulier overwhelmed with his two TV projects, it was often very special.

Coulier has vividly remembered the times he would fly to Detroit to visit his younger sister who was hospitalized and dying of cancer. Alanis liked to come down to meet him, and help cheer her up.

"She really helped my family through a very hard time," Coulier has explained. "Alanis would even visit at the hospital when I wasn't around. My other sister told me once, 'We'll always think so much of that girl because of what she did for my sister. She would always tell me Alanis came by to visit and they sang songs together.' This was happening right when she had maybe a month left, and she would tell us that they were some of the happiest times of her life."

Despite all the warm feelings he had for Alanis, though, the physical distance between the couple created plenty of emotional distance as well. It didn't help any that while he was well established in his career, Alanis was having doubts about hers. She was always "trying to dig deeper into herself, to move toward a more introspective point of view in her music," Coulier has recalled.

By early 1993, the romance ended for reasons that neither of them shared with the outside world. That might explain why a few years later there would be plenty of never-confirmed rumors that Coulier was, in fact, the inspiration for "You Oughta Know."

This was perhaps Alanis's most public, serious relationship up to that point in her life. Whether or not this breakup planted the seed that would grow into her bitter anthem for abandoned lovers everywhere, her experiences with Coulier did fit in quite well with the now-familiar pattern of older men playing a dominant role in her life and career. Finally, she was starting to recognize the trend.

"I was always trying to please everyone," Alanis would explain later, as she reminisced about this period. "Not just boyfriends, but platonic friends, and producers, too. . . . I decided it wasn't just the men, it was something in me too."

A large part of her problem, as she slowly began to realize, was a hole in her self-esteem so large you could drive a semitruckload of therapists through it. It's hard to have any kind of life when you're not certain of who you are and what you really want to do. Sure, she'd come a long way at a relatively young age, which required plenty of strong will and independence, but at the same time, she was surrounded by people telling her what to do. Right down to which heels to wear and how much cleavage to show. Slowly, the doubts began creeping into her mind. Her life had become the property of everyone else around her.

"She's got the record company and [other] people telling her 'you've got to be thinner, you've got to look better. We want you to look like a little pop queen,' " her friend Reny has said. "They want everybody to have boob jobs and be skinny and beautiful . . . you have to be so-o-o self-confident to get over that."

These teen years were not always a negative experience, of course. The attention had its rewards. Still, like so many child stars, so much emphasis had been placed on her bubble-gum image that she was losing touch with who she really wanted to be both personally and musically. There was this creation known as Alanis, the high-heeled, blow-dried dance diva, who probably wouldn't have spent five minutes talking to Alanis Morissette, the high school graduate searching for her own identity. The former existed only to entertain the public, the latter longed for someone with whom she could have some lengthy intellectual intercourse.

"My public musical performing self and my personal intellectual communicative self were completely different. I spent so much time having the two worlds and keeping them separate, and I realized not only how frustrating that was but how unfulfilling that was," she would later explain.

She wanted to express her own opinions, her own frustrations with life, and the vehicle for this would be her sophomore CD. Alanis decided to record once again with Leslie Howe producing, just as he had on *Alanis*. They went to work at Howe's Distortion Studios, with Alanis determined to show more of her true self both musically and lyrically. It was a tough tightrope she had decided to walk. She wanted to make the disc more reflective, more personal but at the same time, her public was expecting another sugary collection of dance-pop hits. Alanis was ready to bare her soul. Her fans wanted to hear heavily synthesized dance music that often seemed devoid of any real emotion.

Actually, neither Howe nor Alanis saw this as that big a leap. They both agreed that the new disc would be less disco-oriented and more serious. It would be a showcase for Alanis's songwriting abilities and not her big hair and fancy outfits. Her second release was to be her way of proving that there really was a brain behind the bump-and-grind of her previous hits. Alanis and Howe worked hard during the spring and summer of 1992, eventually taking nearly eight months to come up with what they figured was the perfect balance of intelligent words and bubbly beats. They could give the fans what they wanted but at the same time start building for the future, allowing Alanis the chance to delve into deeper, more adult material.

She took only one significant break during the recording, returning for a very brief time to her acting roots. In the summer of 1992, she went to Vancouver to film what amounted to a cameo appearance in *Just One of the Girls*, a made-for-TV movie starring another teen hero, Corey Haim. It was the sort of production that made *You Can't Do That on Television* seem like *Masterpiece Theater*. The plot was a predictable bit of fluff about a high school–age musician who is in trouble with a bully and who ends up dressing in drag to avoid a beating and to get close to the girl he is in love with. Kind of a *Some Like It Hot* story with *Saved by the Bell* acting.

Alanis played a singer not coincidentally named Alanis, who appears only briefly in the film near the very end. That's when she gets to sing and dance her way through a flashy stage production of one of the three songs she co-wrote for it, while Haim pounds away at the keyboards as a member of her fictitious band. The bad news for Alanis fans was that in the end, she had barely five minutes of screen time. The good news for Alanis was that she had barely five minutes of screen time. *Just One of the Girls* aired on the Fox network in the United States before disappearing into the land of home video, for which Alanis was no doubt grateful. It shouldn't be surprising that a few years later, when the movie comes up in conversation with an interviewer, she dismisses it as ''horrible'' and the conversation shifts quickly back to her musical career.

Which, luckily, seemed to be moving along much better. Satisfied with the songs she, Howe, and cowriter Cote had come up with, they released her sophomore CD, *Now Is the Time*, in October. The differences between her first and follow-up album were immediately evident. The cover of *Alanis* had featured her as the pouty pubescent with the sexy stare. The front of *Now Is the Time*, on the other hand, had a more subtle photograph. In stark black and white, it is an extreme close-up of the left side of a face. If it weren't for her eyes, revealed beneath a pair of sunglasses pulled down ever-so-slightly, it would be tough to even recognize the singer.

Whereas the artwork in her debut had tried to create some sort of tough mall chick attitude for Alanis, all teased hair and leather, *Now Is the Time* attempted to warm her up a bit and show off her sensitive side. The photos were softer, with Alanis looking pensive and never facing the camera directly. The first disc was as much about image as it was about the material. The second seemed to be trying to deglamorize its creator a bit. The change was by no means drastic, but it was certainly enough to make it clear something slightly different was going on this time around.

The CD jacket even begins with a message from Alanis to those same fans she had gushed to months earlier with her postcard from the Junos. Much of it seemed more like some sort of pop psychology self-help seminar, but it was certainly a step up from the simplistic, transparent emotions expressed on her first disc.

"No regrets. Growth. Give yourself credit," she wrote. "Everybody is different. Their view of you may not be correct. Does it really matter? Who matters? You. Who do you love? What do you know that no one else knows? Take a chance. . . . Learn, learn about you. Be aware. Be positive. Be hopeful. Don't ever let anyone destroy who you are and what you believe. . . ."

These may not be the sort of insights that would make her the next Springsteen, or even the next Stevie Nicks, but they did show a seventeen-year-old girl trying to mature into something beyond the fluffy, boy-crazy kid of *Alanis*. It was a perfectly natural progression. Though she was frozen in the public's mind as an innocent young pop star, she was doing what every kid who bought the first CD was doing—growing up and finally developing some independence from adults. Maybe this wasn't anything approaching the level of eloquence she was able to tap into while writing the songs for *Jagged Little Pill*, but it was another small step away from the old dressed-to-thrill teen dream persona.

Her lyrics on *Now Is the Time* still largely revolved around the same issue that concerned her primary audience—the pursuit of boys—and the music mostly still bumped along with the impersonal, synthesized bop of disco. This time around, though, there were more ballads to soften the mood, along with the occasional moments where you could hear Alanis finally feeling free enough to let loose and let the world know that there was a thinking, feeling young woman behind the bouncy beats.

In the album opener, "Real World," she proudly proclaims that she is ready to make some changes in how the public perceives her. And, more importantly, in how she perceives herself. She decides things for herself "with no one else believin' me" in this ode to self-affirmation. Maybe not the deepest revelation in the world, but quite profound and important for somebody who had spent her life up to that point largely having others tell her what to do and what to be.

Then there's "The Time of Your Life," a smoldering rock tune in which Alanis gleefully tells a reluctant love, "I'm a girl that some may preconceive." When she gets to the chorus, she practically snarls that she's not quite the date her mate figured her to be.

For every moment like "Big Bad Love," in which she reverts to her old teen dance queen mode with cheesy lines like, "I'm having dreams in the night of you," there are other signs Alanis was moving in the direction *she* wanted to go in. Even the otherwise routine, Madonna-like ballad, "(Change Is) Never a Waste of Time," was a billboard for self-esteem, as she cautions a hurt lover not to linger around "for someone who can take all your fear away."

Now Is the Time might not have been the disc Alanis was born to make, but she figured it was at the very least a step toward the respectability that had eluded her with her first release. She wanted to prove to herself that she was capable of putting something more than just a funky little groove into her songs. It was important to let her adoring public understand that despite the cool, calculated sound she was known for, a human heart was beating and a mind was thinking.

At the same time, though, the "business" in "music business" is there for a reason. If you don't sell records, you don't get to make more records. So, in a battle between making art and making commerce, the latter would have to end up the winner. The pressure was on to sell as many records as she had the first time out.

"I myself, as a person, have changed the last couple of years, and I wanted to reflect that, though I didn't want [the CD] to be like the Alanis Diary," she told a journalist while promoting *Now Is the Time*. "It's hard not to think of how commercial you want to be, but then I just don't want to keep writing all kinds of commercial songs and writing for radio and writing for other people."

At first, her fans seemed to approve of her new, more self-assured approach. She flew back to Europe again, to

Rome this time, in order to film a video for the first single, "An Emotion Away," and the song immediately started climbing the charts. It zipped past releases from the more established likes of Bon Jovi, U2, and the Tragically Hip.

She also got back out there to plug her record with the same journalists who had not been particularly big fans of *Alanis*, and many of them noticed right away that something was different about the teenager.

"She was a little more interesting than most [of her peers]," recalls James Muretich, who covers music for the Calgary *Herald* and interviewed Alanis for both her first and her second releases. "She certainly had her own personality and wasn't just some music industry creation, at least the second time around. The first time, she was nice and polite to talk to. The second time, she had become quite flirtatious. It struck me that she had grown up a bit, and her sexuality was more pronounced."

She admitted to him in their 1992 interview that perhaps she had played too safe and slick on her first album, but considered *Now Is the Time* to be "a happy medium" between getting deeper with her music and giving people what they wanted, which was essentially a replay of the first disc. She was trying to slowly head off along a road of her own, but when she looked behind her, nobody was following. The CD would eventually sell about fifty thousand copies, a respectable amount but a huge disappointment when compared to the mammoth success Alanis had enjoyed just a year earlier with her debut. The reviews, what there were of them anyway, were relatively respectable.

"People were mostly kind to her," says Muretich. "I didn't want to dump on her. There were no raves, but I did recognize that she was trying to do something more."

Nonetheless, the disc sputtered out and slid right off the charts. Even worse, just as with *Alanis*, she made virtually no money on *Now Is the Time*. Much of the advance she and Howe had received they had poured into the making of the disc, and her deal with MCA didn't call for any royalties. Fame, she had now discovered, didn't automatically come with fortune attached.

Howe has recalled that the music was trapped somewhere in musical limbo between pop and dance. Despite his and Alanis's pride in the emotions and insights the songs contained, the clubbing crowd didn't want to dance to the more subdued beats and the Top 40 types apparently preferred something lighter and happier, which left the disc up a creek without a fan. Even her former supporters at MuchMusic balked at putting the video for "Real World" into their regular rotation. According to Cote, it was rejected because "the song was reflective of her new attitude and the video was considered violent. The attitude was, 'Where is our sweet little Alanis?' Here they have this young artist, and then she throws some rocks around."

He realized that the first album had been made for a younger audience, but nobody could be sure whether that group had grown up and thought of Alanis as kid stuff now, or she had disappointed her faithful by doing the growing up herself. Whatever the case, the record started up the charts and then disappointed everyone involved by just stopping dead.

More than likely, it was just the natural way of the music business that had done her in. Teenage dance kings and queens are like some new breakfast cereal. They're all sugary-sweet, use fancy packaging to lure in a young clientele and, once that audience is done digesting their empty calories, it's time to move on to the next slick package. Today's Tiffany or Debbie Gibson or New Kids on the Block is tomorrow's twenty-five-cent special at every yard sale in town. Raise your hand if you still own a Vanilla Ice CD.

It was also a case of bad timing. *Now Is the Time* was really a misnomer. The timing of its release couldn't have been worse. Late 1992 was an era when lightweight, danceable pop music had fallen out of favor everywhere. The CD had come along just as Nirvana and Pearl Jam and a host of other bands were popularizing the grunge sound, a dark, introspective style that was to Alanis's music what Franz

Kafka's books are to Danielle Steele's. The greatest trauma in her material usually was breaking up with a guy. The greatest trauma in grunge, meanwhile, was a complete loss of faith in humanity. Pessimism and anger, two feelings Alanis never expressed in her songs, had become fashionable.

It wasn't just the music that had changed, either. All the aesthetic touches that Alanis was equally known for had become exceedingly unhip. Flannel shirts replaced leather jackets. Doc Martens boots replaced designer heels. Nose and navel rings replaced hoop earrings. You didn't poof up your hair anymore. You shaved it all off. Dressing down-and-out was all the rage now, and Alanis just appeared out of touch with the trend. And in popular music, trendiness is next to godliness. Time had not only passed Alanis by, it had run over her and kept on going.

So there she was, only eighteen and not even a year removed from her shining moment at the Junos, and she had already become a golden oldie. She could stay secure in her career, with her songwriting deal with MCA Publishing in Canada still intact. MCA's Alexander had been her supporter all along, firmly believing in her talent. Even if her record hadn't sold well, he looked at the situation as a temporary setback. He still strongly believed in her songwriting abilities. And unfazed by his phenom's fading fan base in her homeland, Alexander looked to the United States as an untapped market. Her albums had never been released south of the border, so why not give them a shot at success in the States. Americans liked Canada's beer and its bacon, so why wouldn't they go for its dance darling?

In early 1993, Alexander contacted the Los Angeles–based Atlas/Third Rail Management, looking for some help to boost Alanis's sagging career. He was after Scott Welch, a partner in the business and a former road manager and sound engineer, whose most noticeable career achievement had been helping transform former Los Angeles Lakers cheerleader/choreographer Paula Abdul into one of the best-selling dance acts of the late 1980s. If he could work that miracle with someone who had only a limited musical background, just imagine what he could do with someone like Alanis.

Alexander sent Alanis's two discs to Welch, who, while impressed by what he heard, held off on expressing any interest in the singer. Instead, he arranged a dinner meeting with Alanis in New York a few weeks later. By the time dessert arrived, he was completely captivated by her. He returned to Los Angeles. She went back to Ottawa. And they continued to speak on the phone on a regular basis, feeling each other out. Welch sensed something much different in Alanis, something that had nothing to do with her obvious musical gifts.

Welch realized quickly that Alanis's early success had left her frustrated. She had more talent than her prefabricated sound and image had allowed, but she had never had the opportunity to relax and nurture her abilities. Though she was not yet a great musician, he felt, she had plenty of ideas and just needed time to concentrate on sorting them out. Instead of licensing her first two albums for U.S. release, which would essentially put her right back where she started, he set to work helping her develop a master plan for an entirely new career as an adult.

The first thing that had to be done was to let her ditch the teen dance queen persona that just didn't seem to fit her anymore. That meant Klovan and Howe were the odd men out. Along with D'Arcy, they were the ones who'd helped craft the image she now seemed to be distancing herself from. The little girl willing to do whatever others told her she needed to do if she wanted to build her career was maturing into an independent thinker who realized she must experience life and music on her own terms for a change.

It's not that life in Ottawa was horrible. Alanis still had her family to support her, and plenty of friends to hang out with. She did perform every once in a while, like the time in late 1992 when Cote and his novelty-rock band, Joe Gatineau and the Mont-Bleu Rockers, needed a backup singer to perform with them on a local radio broadcast.

''She was there to perform also and said, 'I want to sing

with you,' " says Cote. "We did 'Little Drummer Boy' and in the middle of it, our singer started ad-libbing this silly story. I still have the tape of that night, and all you can hear is Alanis laughing in the background so hard, she could barely breathe."

Not long after that, she was at a local television station, helping out with a telethon to support Ottawa's Children's Hospital, a facility she used to perform at when she was younger. Alanis was one of the local celebrities invited to come on and take calls from citizens phoning in pledges. Her old teacher, MacGregor, came by the studio to see if he could go on the air to pledge $100 in honor of a friend's young daughter who had recently passed away. The station wouldn't commit to letting him on-camera, but as he was leaving, MacGregor happened to run into Alanis and Georgia.

"I asked if Alanis could get me on, and then went home," he recalls. "This was about 9 P.M., and at about midnight, the phone rang. It was Georgia. She told me that if I got there right away, Alanis had arranged a spot for me to go on. That was great."

He would not see her again for quite some time. She was preparing to leave town. Alanis had the opportunity to go to college once her days at Glebe were done; she was accepted at the University of Ottawa, the University of Toronto, and Carleton University in Ottawa, but she never matriculated at any of them. Instead, career won out once again. She listened to Welch's and Alexander's advice, and decided to pack her bags for an educational stay in Toronto that didn't involve any school, except perhaps the ever-popular School of Hard Knocks. Welch had a plan. Let his new client get out on her own and take in some new surroundings. Experiencing life solo for a while would allow her writing to find the personal edge it was lacking.

Most of her life had been spent pursuing her dream of being in show business, and she'd never really taken time out to live in the normal, work-a-day world people who buy CDs came from. If she was ever going to take a long, hard look at herself and discover what it was she really wanted to write, this was the time and Toronto was the place. A firm believer in what she would later refer to as "that whole concept of having to hit rock bottom in order to make any changes," Alanis set about reorganizing a life that had slipped away from her.

Four

The idea was simple. She wouldn't be Alanis anymore. She'd be Casper. A ghost. Invisible. Out of sight, at least when she chose to be. She'd live in Toronto, commute back home as often as possible to see her family, and for the first time in her young life, take time to simply focus on the craft of her songwriting rather than on doing whatever it took for people to notice her.

It was a good choice. She could have rushed to one of the two most obvious cities, New York or Los Angeles, both big hubs of the music business. Neither seemed quite right, because they were too big and too distracting. They were precisely the sort of places where somebody who didn't know where she fit into that business must avoid. Toronto, on the other hand, was a laid-back, artsy, relatively wholesome town despite its population of nearly 700,000. It had all sorts of natural beauty, from its parks to the view of Lake Ontario, and a thriving artistic community.

Whether it was the numerous musical festivals, the volume of film and television production that made Toronto North America's third largest film and video production center, or the three hundred clothing and textile firms that had turned fashion into a major local industry, Toronto presented the perfect environment for someone looking to expand her creativity.

Alanis took a mouse-infested, third-floor walk-up apartment in the city's Beaches district, a fashionable and artsy enclave located on the shores of Lake Ontario. It was a far cry from the glitz and glamour of her previous big trip to Toronto for the Junos. Now, instead of soaking up the adulation, she was trying to get it out of her system.

"I saw how unfulfilling it was—the whole fame, celebrity part [of life]," she later explained. "That's why the best thing I ever did was just walk away and start over. In those days, I wrote music to entertain people as opposed to communicate with them."

As far as she was concerned, that meant putting an end to her days of trying to please everyone else and instead trying to please herself. That meant spending more time cultivating her love life. At nineteen, she lost her virginity, the good little Catholic girl holding out as long as she could despite living a life she would later look back on as "deviant and perverse." In particular, she had developed a bad habit of stealing other girls' boyfriends, just to prove that she could.

"The only way I felt desirable was when a man would leave his girlfriend for me. I wish I could go back and apologize to all the girls I did that to," she later told an interviewer. "And if I ever dated guys my own age, it would only last about a week."

She may have discovered sex, but real romance continued to elude her. So, after what seemed to her to have been "the twentieth bad relationship," she opted to steer as clear of romance as she could in order to focus on the job at hand. Writing music.

It was a very gradual process. Her management encouraged her to work with other writers, and one of the projects she decided to participate in was a program called Song Works, run by peermusic, a publishing house with offices in both Los Angeles and Toronto. One of the program's unique traits was the once-a-month seven P.M. meetings, where all those wanting to participate would show up and put their names on slips of paper tossed into a hat. All the musicians, usually about fourteen, would sip coffee and chat for a while until it was time to get to work. Then, everyone would pull out a name and spend the next few weeks in a partnership alongside whomever fate had thrown them together with.

There were no musical prejudices in the group. Writers from all different genres—country, folk, rock, pop—participated in the project, and once they were paired up, the idea was to finish a song and perhaps even record a demo tape by the time of the next class. More importantly, though, Song Works was there to create a support network for Toronto musicians, giving them a sounding board for their new material. That meant instant camaraderie for Alanis. David Baxter, a fellow songwriter who was the creative director for peermusic's Canadian office, had some knowledge of his new participant's disco days, but didn't really care what sort of tunes she used to do. He had met her briefly during that period of her life and came away thinking, " 'That's somebody!' It was something about her vibe."

MCA Publishing had referred Alanis to Song Works, and Baxter was very eager to have her join in. Despite her relative recent fame, he recalls, nobody in the program really seemed to recognize her. And she didn't do anything to prompt their memories. She would often show up in a floral dress, looking very conservative, acting very respectful of the others but also confident of her own talents. "She never talked about the old years," says Steve Haflidson, who wrote with Alanis after drawing her name from the hat. "She was quiet . . . more prim and proper, very suburban."

So, step number one in Operation Toronto was a success. Alanis had managed to shed her old image and landed in a place where she could be judged strictly on the music she was going to make, rather than the material she had already done. From the first day she participated, she was a hit with her peers. She had to be, since she ended up working with plenty of them. According to Haflidson, who continues to write and perform in the Toronto area and recently recorded a solo album to be released independently, those who wrote with Alanis had a nickname for themselves. They began jokingly referring to themselves as a support group called "the Alanis 100," because that's about how many collaborators she eventually had.

"She was an awesome singer, with accuracy and confidence," says Baxter, who still works for peermusic in Toronto. "And she was a remarkably hard worker. She just got up in the morning and made it happen."

Though some might join in the program to show off their flashy playing technique, Alanis was different. She and Baxter coined the phrase "lick-free zone" for Song Works, which meant "not wanking, just playing the song," he says. Alanis proved so dedicated and talented, she became very popular in the group. So popular, in fact, it was soon hard to get an appointment if you wanted to try your hand at writing with her.

She'd be off "practicing keyboards at one place, then working with another person the next afternoon," says Baxter, who did manage to try working on songs with his young charge. They'd sit together, trying to hammer out a tune, and Baxter would look over to see her singing a new melody and illustrating it with her hand as if she were a conductor. For a brief time, he also tried to teach her how to play the guitar, but it became evident that "she had such a facility for melody, she didn't need it" to help her.

Tim Thorney, another veteran Canadian singer/songwriter, took a turn penning a few tunes with Alanis, and found the experience to be more like attending a concert. His sessions with her were more like "writing performances. We'd tape everything we did and somewhere in there, she would give an entire performance. [The talent] just fell off of her."

Another one of her cowriters, Arlene Bishop, was amazed by one of Alanis's other unique habits. When the two of them worked together, Alanis was never without her little hand-held tape recorder.

"We'd write something, and wade through all the nonsense to get to a good idea, then she'd stop and say, 'Hold on!' Then she'd sing the line into the tape recorder so we could remember it later," says Bishop, who now records as a solo artist for Universal Records in Canada.

As they wrote, Alanis would often tell Bishop that she wished she could be as tough as her songwriting pal, and that in turn inspired Bishop to work harder at their music. She was in awe of how deep this girl not even old enough to drink yet could go with her material. Baxter also couldn't help but notice how devoted Alanis was to her lyrics, and the way she was trying hard to put as much of her life experiences into them. *Jagged Little Pill* wouldn't start coming together for more than a year, but the seeds for the disc were being sown during this time.

"She was standing right next to her idea," Baxter says. "It was getting closer and closer. She was ready to express real emotion, and didn't want to do silly little pop songs anymore."

She wanted to keep her songs personal, instead of tackling big issues. It was the personal politics that interested her. And everyone in her new social circle represented a case study. As impressed as they were by her musical abilities, many were even more taken by her inquisitive personality. She was part musician, part therapist. Baxter got to be close friends with her, and they would often go out for coffee to talk about music ("She knew a lot about music history") or, more importantly, Baxter's love life.

"She was always giving me advice about the mess that was my personal life," recalls Baxter. "If ever there was proof that somebody was an old soul, she was it."

The teenager seldom offered up news of her own romantic crises, and although there were stories about a long-term relationship that was turning sour, she kept her writing partners in the dark about what was really happening. Instead, she turned the tables in personal conversations, fishing for information about them.

"She was interested in gossipy stuff. I was getting engaged and she wanted to hear all about it. She was always interested in people's feelings," Haflidson says.

Some things never change. She was not even twenty yet, but still acting like the grown-up around others. Baxter can still recall the night income tax forms needed to be filed, and at five minutes before the filing deadline of midnight, Alanis was rushing him to the post office to mail five years' worth of tax returns. Naturally, she had already taken care of her own.

As friendly as she was to some of her fellow writers, though, something didn't seem right. Haflidson had noticed that she seemed "restless, and you knew that this wasn't for her." The ultimate goal in a class full of songwriters is to come up with material that would sell. That's their job. It was different for Alanis. She had already written songs that sold by the bucketload. Her desire was to create music that meant something to her, and then see if anybody in the outside world wanted to listen to it.

Most of her new acquaintances couldn't tell that anything was seriously wrong. She came to parties at their homes. She kept up a positive attitude about her work. "She didn't come across as miserable. She was always alert and up," says Haflidson.

Still, on many evenings, she'd find herself sitting alone on a rock that gave her a beautiful view of Lake Ontario, staring into space and contemplating the troubles in what she would later call "the hardest time in my whole life." The combination of boy trouble and her inability to find a cowriter with whom she really clicked left her feeling miserable inside, and she preferred to think things through on her own, out there on the rock. She was an expert at keeping those around her from knowing how troubled she felt. ("We had so much fun. It didn't seem like she was having a bad time," says Tim Thorney.)

That's not to say there weren't a few moments during the Song Works days when things really seemed to work. In particular, there was the evening she performed with Haflidson on a tune of his called "Gone." Like most of his material, it had a country-folky feel to it. Not Alanis's usual style, but something she was more than happy to try out. The result was a stirring, soul-searing version of a bittersweet song that left everyone in the Song Works room amazed by what they had just heard.

"People got goosebumps listening to her," recalls Baxter.

"Everyone was bowled over," adds Haflidson. "She was right there with the song. There was no doubt about what was going on with her talent. David [Baxter] came up to the front of the room and said, 'If MCA ever lets her go, I know others who would be interested in her.'"

They thought the world of her and her work. Alanis, however, had spent so much of her career working with older musicians to whom she felt emotionally incompatible, she had lost some confidence in her own abilities. Without a cowriter, she feared at some level, maybe she would fall flat on her face and nobody would pick her back up.

Now she was having doubts about ever finding a partner who understood what she was trying to do. There may have been an occasional spark or two when writing with someone in Toronto, but no four-alarm fires. She continued to work hard at her craft, writing seven days a week whether it was by herself or with mates from Song Works, but the frustration continued to build.

She wasn't helping herself much when she had a career relapse and, despite her manager's plan to ease her out of her dance days and into something more meaningful, she found herself booked on a New Year's Eve special airing in the last hours of 1993, broadcast live all around Canada from Niagara Falls. Why did she agree to do this? Wasn't it a step backward, precisely the sort of thing she'd come to Toronto to get away from? Who knows? Perhaps this was her way of living out that old saying, "Whatever doesn't kill you makes you stronger—because this performance was deadly.

She should have known it would be a long evening when even a pseudo hip-hop group called MMC, a.k.a. the new Mickey Mouse Club (which might explain why their music sounded snow white), got more time on stage than she did. Even worse, when it was time to do her first song, Alanis had to come out in the freezing weather, looking all nicely pressed in a black sportcoat and pants with a bright red scarf, to sing to a recorded backing track of "Real World." Gigs don't get much worse than this. The crowd milled about, paying her little attention. The tune began with roadies out on the stage setting up for the next act. Her mike didn't work at first, and then her voice struggled to stay on key during the opening verse. Alanis tried hard, smiling and trying to pump up the crowd with her buoyant attitude, but nothing worked. It was a relief for everyone when the tape of her song ended and she was free to exit the stage.

Much later in the show, Alanis got another shot to perform. This time, singing "Give What You Got" from *Now Is the Time*, at least a band backed her up. They didn't look particularly excited to be there, but they were there. Her voice was now present and accounted for. The crowd had gotten drunker, so people in the audience seemed to be enjoying themselves more. Still, part of the song was obscured by feedback from the sound system, and her dance gyrations at the edge of the stage looked kind of stiff and silly. Urging the crowd to "turn to the person next to you and kiss them" also came across as a rather forced comment. She kept smiling gamely, but it became readily apparent that this persona was just that. A persona. It wasn't something she seemed comfortable with, no matter how hard she tried. The fact that audiences seemed more infatuated with the new Mickey Mouse Club, which came across as a bunch of kids watering down the beats of rap and hiphop music until it was as threatening as tapioca pudding, was another bad sign.

If there was any consolation, at least this was the final death knell for Disco Alanis. It was apparent to anyone who watched her that night how unnatural the whole persona was. So, as 1994 rolled in, she was continuing to branch out on her own. She briefly returned to television, this time hosting a Canadian Broadcasting Corporation show called *Music Works*. A twist on the *MTV Unplugged* fad, this program had performers doing a handful of songs in front of a live audience that had been tucked inside an Ottawa warehouse studio space. The music was not always performed acoustically, but the surroundings were designed to give it a raw edge the artists couldn't find in a more traditional setting.

Now this was something that could do her image some good. Not only were the show's performers given a chance to get down-and-dirty, so was the host. Just being there gave her legitimacy. In the meantime, though, she kept pushing herself to find a cowriter who could sense how personal she wanted her music to be. She had been encouraged by her management to start looking outside Toronto for cowriters, and that had meant a side trip first to Nashville in 1993 and then, not long after her New Year's Eve performance, to Los Angeles.

Considering her musical history, Nashville seemed an odd choice. Alanis was about as country as Tammy Wynette was heavy metal. However, if she was going to truly move away from her pop princess past, trying something this different made sense. Working with writers who preferred a folk or country approach, like Bishop or Haflidson, had helped give her a taste of something new.

As for Los Angeles, it was inevitable she would eventually wind up there. It has long been the unofficial headquarters for the music industry. That's where the record companies are. That's where the writers are. Most importantly, although she didn't know it at the time, that's where Glen Ballard is.

MCA Publishing, for whom Ballard also wrote, set up a meeting at his home studio in February 1994. Alanis had been through plenty of these musical blind dates already. You sit down and talk to another songwriter. You realize what it is you're both trying to accomplish. Then, if you've made it this far, you spend time writing together. And after that fails, you start all over again. There was no reason for either of them to assume this session would be anything different, and Ballard would later admit that he took the meeting simply because he was "not uninterested" in meeting this unknown talent from Canada.

He already had a pretty full plate. Ballard had begun his career in the Elton John organization, eventually working his way up to playing piano for one of John's protégés, Kiki Dee. This work had led him to a gig writing for MCA Publishing, with artists such as George Benson recording his material. That in turn enabled him to meet Quincy Jones, who became a mentor to the mild-mannered songwriter from Natchez, Mississippi. His first big break, writing a song for Michael Jackson's *Thriller*, turned out to be a bust when it was cut from the final product.

However, Jones continued to work with Ballard and when it came time for Jackson to record his follow-up album, *Dangerous*, Ballard did manage to get a song on this time. It was "Man in the Mirror," one of the singer's biggest hits ever. Not only did Ballard earn plenty of accolades for that song, he also started up a producing career, which would eventually lead him to work on hit albums by the likes of Wilson Phillips, Van Halen, and Aerosmith.

This was one busy guy, and at first his encounter with Alanis seemed like it would be business as usual for her. Here she was, now nineteen and going to work once again with an older male career musician. Her previous pattern was repeating itself. Still, she and Ballard did have a few things in common that set this partnership apart from her past writing relationships. They both had taken an interest in music very early in their lives, with Ballard actually writing his first song at age five. He used to pester his family by performing tunes for them, just as Alanis had done when she was very young. He grew up in a Catholic family, just as she had. By the mid-1980s, he had moved to Los Angeles and worked his way up through the music business, developing a reputation as a purveyor of slick and lightweight pop and R&B tunes. Not unlike the reputation a young Alanis had developed thanks to her two albums.

Despite the similarities, however, it was hard to imagine that these two might click creatively. He was forty-one and she was still only nineteen. Ballard had been married to wife Liv for fourteen years and had two young sons, and Alanis was steadfastly single and continually unlucky in love. She wanted to search for her soul in her music, and he had written supremely saccharine semi-soulful tunes like

Jackson's "Man in the Mirror." They were a truly odd couple in many ways, but the moment she set foot in the second-floor studio and plopped down in the comfy couch there, both of their lives changed forever.

"Glen had a certain history, as I had, and when we met, we immediately connected. We just started with a clean slate," Alanis would later explain.

They sat down, had a cup of tea, and within an hour were working on a song. And by the end of the day, they'd finished the tune. Back in Toronto, she labored every day of the week to come up with something that pleased her. Now, in just one day, she had discovered how to let herself go and get in touch with what it was she really wanted to communicate in her music. Instead of being afraid to express her own emotions, she now couldn't stop them from spilling out all over the floor of Ballard's studio.

"It was an immediate chemistry, personally and creatively," Ballard has said. "I just liked her a lot. She was curious and, intellectually, she was articulate, self-possessed, and very bright. She was only nineteen but I thought I was talking to a thirty-year-old. There was no sense that she was one age and I was another. We just hit it off. At that moment I had still not heard a note of music and didn't know what she wanted to do."

She wasn't entirely certain either, but, together, they would soon find out.

Five

*E*ncino—an upper middle-class Los Angeles suburb that has the pleasant, homey, white-bread feel of a TV sit-com. If this peaceful neighborhood were to produce a record, you'd think it would have to be something involving the Brady Bunch. The houses are big but not Beverly Hills big. The lawns are well manicured, but not showy. The streets are clean and wide and without any foot traffic.

It also happens to be the home of Glen Ballard, whose understated two-story home features such wholesome touches as a small garden in the front and a basketball hoop in the driveway. Only when you get upstairs do things start to look somewhat different. The hallways are lined with gold records and framed articles, mementos of a life spent in popular music. Tucked in one corner of the second floor is a surprisingly tiny room—certainly no bigger than 450 square feet—that gets flooded with sunlight every day. The place is filled with guitars and keyboards and several pieces of space-age-looking recording equipment. There is also a small recording booth against one wall, and a well-worn couch alongside another.

This certainly doesn't look like the kind of place music history could be made, yet it is where one of the most significant records of the past decade was born. This is where Alanis and Ballard sat together, hammering out the songs that would become *Jagged Little Pill*.

From the moment they met, she had known she wanted to keep working with him. Ballard was the one person she'd come across in more than a year who really understood what she was trying to do. Many of her other cowriters were well intentioned, but couldn't provide a spark.

So in June of 1994, just a few months after their first meeting, Alanis made another trip south of the border to work with Ballard. Over the course of their three weeks together, they really started to push themselves, and these sessions led to the birth of *Jagged Little Pill* numbers like "Perfect" and "Ironic."

It was as if her creativity had finally found a home in Ballard's cozy studio, not to mention Los Angeles itself. And if she felt at home there, she might as well actually get a home in the City of Angels. It was time. Although she would continue to return to Canada to visit old friends and family, the Toronto phase of her life had essentially come to an end.

When she made it clear that it was time she moved on, there weren't any hard feelings among her soon-to-be-former songwriting companions. They just didn't quite know what to make of her plans. She may have been feeling more confident about her writing thanks to her time with Ballard, but there was no reason to think she'd fare any better in the States than she had been during the past year in Canada.

"I remember meeting her at a party after she'd made the decision to move," recalls Haflidson. "I told her, 'I hope we don't read about you turning tricks down there or anything.' "

She'd let out a pleasant laugh at the good-natured jibe. Nobody really knew what would happen to her after she left, least of all Alanis herself, but it was important to keep up a sense of humor about the whole move. Sure it was risky, but only by taking chances could she truly test herself and her abilities. Maybe this whole plan wouldn't work out.

Maybe all the creativity now flowing through her veins as a result of her collaboration with Ballard was only temporary.

Still, she'd never know if she didn't take the chance. Alanis had come to Toronto to figure out her life and career, to forget about what had been and concentrate on what could be. She'd been able to do plenty of the former, but the lack of a satisfactory collaborator meant there was little chance for the latter. No, she had to take the next step forward, to a city and a country where she would be a complete unknown, finally learning how to let loose the songs that had been in her heart for a very long time.

Like Ballard's neighborhood, his house, and his studio, the way the pair worked was deceptively simple. Alanis would sit on the floor or on the couch, and Ballard would take out a guitar to try out a few licks while she let her pen flow across sheets of paper. Or she'd start singing. This proved to be "the most spiritual experience either of us ever had with music," she would later say. "The whole thing was very accelerated and stream-of-consciousness."

Perhaps for the first time ever in her career, Alanis was closing in on her true musical self. Here, even less than in Toronto during the past year, there was nobody to tell her no. Nobody to insist that she go for the hit single instead of taking her songs one level deeper.

Least of all Glen Ballard who encouraged her to find her voice. The quintessential quiet Southern gentleman, he was able to truly listen to what Alanis was struggling to say. "What makes this relationship so magic for me is that a lot of what I would be talking about or thinking about or intellectualizing about . . . Glen would say, 'Well, yeah?' to when most people would be, 'What are you talking about?' or 'God, would you stop analyzing!' We'd talk and out of the conversation would come a song."

It was always just the two of them up there in the studio, working twelve- to sixteen-hour days, starting in late morning and finishing up in the wee hours of the following day, with only a brief lunch and dinner break at a nearby Italian restaurant for her favorite meal, the chopped salad. They'd usually begin their sessions just sitting and chatting, and that would eventually segue into music.

Alanis would go into the recording booth and, with Ballard's musical accompaniment, get a rough version on tape of whatever tune they'd been experimenting with. By 2 A.M., they'd play it back and, most of the time, enjoy what they were hearing so much that they'd start screaming. Even in such an unpolished form, they could feel the magic of what they were doing.

"We'd look at each other and be . . . giddy," Alanis has said. "Knowing that this thing was real whether people would ever hear it or not. Those were forever the best moments and I crave them again. I miss them."

Ballard would later also reminisce that "we'd literally write and record a song in a day. That process was so much a factor in us capturing the moment."

Jagged Little Pill would eventually include about 80 percent of these original demo tapes because, according to Alanis, "we didn't want to be too precious about it and go through it with a fine-tooth comb or anything." On her earlier recordings, her voice was made to sound flawless during the course of fifteen or twenty takes. This time around, she wanted the recording process to be as spontaneous and honest as what she was trying to sing about.

The songs she and Ballard labored over were meant as an emotional release for her. She was purging all the pain and heartache she'd stored up since her days as a child star, and to go back over each of the songs again and again would dilute their immediacy and honesty. It wasn't until long after she had finished with her writing that she was able to go back and analyze what it was she was trying to do.

"In retrospect, I see that record as a response . . . to what I was immersed in when I was younger; it was a response to society; it was a response to the way I was treated, the way I was brought up. The way I was taught to be," Alanis would eventually observe.

Sure, she was troubled by the thought that some of her lyrics might be *too* honest, at least for those whom they were written about. Nonetheless, she had committed herself to getting all the negative emotions out of her system. There was no stopping now. She was so comfortable working with Ballard that she realized it was time for her to open up her music completely or "at some point I was going to explode . . . or implode."

Instead, the real eruption came with each of the thirteen tunes that wound up on *Jagged Little Pill*. She had created the disc the way some people fill their diaries, and every tune boiled over with one personal revelation after another. It's never been common that we hear songs that are *about* something, that speak directly to the heart instead of numbing the brain with "Oh, baby, baby" platitudes or heavy-handed and artsy (a.k.a. indecipherable) metaphors. Even rarer are emotional, involving lyrics that are irresistible when accompanied by catchy, Top 40–friendly melodies.

But that was precisely what Ballard and Morissette had pieced together. This was an autobiography you could hum along with, a very personal, intimate record with music accessible enough for everyone. "The record is my story," Alanis has said. "I think of the album as running over different facets of my personality."

At last, inside the tiny confines of Ballard's home studio, she was able to stop worrying about what anyone else thought about her words or music or hairstyle or age or anything else. All she had to do was let her mind wander to where it wanted to go. Many times, it even got up and ran there. "Hand in My Pocket," an amiable midtempo tribute to the power of positive thinking was actually written in about fifteen minutes. It also marked Alanis's debut as a harmonica player, and she was so good the first time around, she and Ballard moved on and never went back to do a second take.

"We wrote in a really sort of accelerated kind of way," Alanis later told an interviewer. That meant the writing and recording process was "the shortest amount of time and the most spiritual time that I've ever had in my life, so I'd like to think that now that I've tapped into that way of writing, I'll continue to do that again. . . ."

Discovering this approach didn't come right away. "Hand in My Pocket" actually came about during a period of time when Alanis and Ballard were "having a bit of a dry spell," she has said. He was pacing the floor and she was sitting on the couch, when she decided to write about precisely how she was feeling at that moment in time. Ballard helped find music for this lyrical Polaroid, and the song was done.

This was a perfect example of her new approach to her craft. The songs came so quickly because she wasn't thinking her way through them. She was feeling her way. The process was instinctual, not technical, as it had been when she worked with other collaborators. "Right Through You" is also a product of this emotion-led approach. The song, which rolls in softly and builds to a chorus raucous enough to stun small animals at ten paces, is the revenge of a show-biz kid finally talking back at all the good ol' industry boys who viewed her as "a sweet back-loaded puppet" and their meal ticket.

Listening to musicians sing about how hard the music business is is like hearing a doctor complain about how he blew a putt on the fourteenth hole. They don't really have your sympathy. However, Alanis turned her anti-record-biz tirade into a celebration of self-esteem instead of a tribute to self-pity.

"Everything I write is a particular case," she would later say of the tune. "That song . . . there are about seven people in that one. And a couple of them have asked me if they're in there. Isn't that sad?"

The genteel "Forgiven" grew out of her Catholic upbringing, and the uptight, repressive attitude about sex that comes with such a childhood. Lines like "My brothers they never went blind" for their erotic escapades were clearly the work of someone frustrated by the rigidity and the gender politics that come with organized religion. Even though her parents had allowed her to have a rather liberal upbringing—it's not every mom and dad who let their teenage daughter jet around the world with men twice her age—their Catholicism had left her feeling that something was missing in her life. Namely, sex. It's not that she wasn't sexually active during her teen years. It's just that for every deviant bit of behavior she tried, part of her held back, a slave to the Catholic guilt that had been ingrained in her.

"I had to be this beautiful prize virgin," she has said. "It didn't make any sense. When I was eleven or twelve, I started asking questions—and there never seemed to be any answers. No one could ever tell me why any of this was, so my parents let me make my own decisions. And I strayed away from that. There are a lot of good thoughts [in organized religion], but there is so much repression—and *that's* what set me up for where I was going to come from."

"Mary Jane," a sweet, gentle tune in which the singer offers comfort to a friend who is at the end of her rope, is also firmly based on a real experience. During a coffee break she took while writing *Jagged Little Pill*, Alanis spoke with a friend, who was telling her about everything that was happening in her life. Afterward, Alanis realized that her own most effective way to advise this woman was in a song. A song that was meant to inspire herself as well as her friend.

"In a roundabout way, it's also me singing it to myself real softly, reminding myself what matters," she has said. "I wanted to tell her all this stuff, but I didn't think it would make an impact. So many times, telling people stuff you see or realize doesn't make them change. Listening to them may make them feel better, but it doesn't change anything either. Then sometimes you put it in a song, and they can draw from it what they need."

This desire to offer life lessons to her listeners is also evident in "You Learn," a midtempo number that plays like a self-help book, advising that even getting rejected is a perfect growth experience. Without pain, you couldn't recognize happiness. The tune was a way for her to examine all that had happened to her over the years and to let the world know that "when you're immersed in something painful, you don't realize there's any lesson. A lot of what I wrote about was difficult times from which I walked away a better person.''

Only one song of the thirteen that would eventually make its way onto *Jagged Little Pill*, she has said, was not 100 percent true. Perhaps that explains why the track, ''Your House,'' sung a cappella, would be buried after the twelve tunes that are officially listed on the CD. It features Alanis breaking into an ex-lover's house to play his Joni Mitchell albums and smell his cologne. Even this secret song, though, has one foot in the real world. It was inspired by the time Alanis stayed at the house of a guy upon whom she had a bit of a crush. He let her stay over there while he was gone for a week, and curiosity got the better of her. She decided to sleep in his bed, but the thrill was short-lived because the experience ''was eerie and unnerving.''

Probably the two most important songs to emerge from the Ballard sessions, however, were ''Perfect'' and ''You Oughta Know.'' The former was significant because it was a breakthrough of sorts for Alanis as a songwriter, while the latter would become the tune that broke through to the public. ''Perfect'' came about by accident, suddenly appearing as Alanis and Ballard were halfway into some other song that would never make it onto *Jagged Little Pill*.

The original demo they recorded at one A.M. that day is essentially what can be heard on *Jagged Little Pill*, and was so starkly personal that Alanis just sat there in Ballard's studio until five in the morning ''because . . . it was pretty scary.'' Not surprisingly, she has referred to ''Perfect'' as her breakthrough song. Up until that point, she had been by her own admission a rather analytical person. Everything that had happened in her life and career had to be dissected and studied until it all made sense. With this particular song, however, she ''didn't have any answer'' for how it had spontaneously emerged from somewhere within her psyche.

It doesn't seem that hard to figure out what the inspiration for the tune might have been. With lyrics about making a child what the adult never was, ''Perfect'' is a harsh critique of parents who push their children too far, too fast.

The message from this mother and father is clear: they'd love their kid just a bit more if he or she would just be more, well, perfect. Considering Alanis's life in show business, this seems like a direct assault on Alan and Georgia.

Later, she wouldn't deny that she drew some inspiration for the song from her relationship with her parents. "I have a pretty great family but there's no such thing as a dysfunction-free one, y'know. It's just to what degree. And the song was just sort of my verbalizing . . . the sort of unsaid things that I felt, the pressure that I felt that I could not ever really put my finger on until I wrote this song."

She knew all too well what it felt like to have to play the role of perfect adolescent, a part she had been cast in for years. And it isn't just parents who force their children into such an uncomfortable position. Everyone bears a little bit of the blame, and "Perfect" was Alanis's way of venting about the societal pressures any kid is under, whether he or she is going out for the baseball team or auditioning for "Star Search." "No one ever says those things, but they're intimated everywhere: Unless you are externally successful, you are nothing. I was able to put it into words, what I felt. . . . It was cathartic. That was the turning point."

In particular, it paved the way for what was perhaps *Jagged Little Pill*'s most confessional tune. And the song that would guarantee her plenty of attention when the record was finally released.

The writing of "You Oughta Know" was a deeply revelatory experience that left both her and Ballard amazed at its creation. It was written in the course of one afternoon, when, Alanis has said, she "must have been trying to come to terms with that dysfunctional part of my subconscious." Specifically, the section reserved for dwelling on failed romances. Was it about Dave Coulier? Or perhaps some boyfriend from the old Toronto days? Whoever it was, he certainly had some explaining to do once this tune became popular.

This would become Alanis's most famous—and most misunderstood—song. It is a nasty tirade against an older former lover, and an anthem for anyone who has ever been unceremoniously seduced and abandoned by their own version of her Mr. Duplicity. The power and emotion of the song left many a guy feeling like he'd been smacked in the groin by a ninety mile-an-hour fastball, while women could hear it and simply nod with recognition.

Alanis was frank and to the point, baring all about her own personal proclivities in the process. She sarcastically grills her former mate about what sexual favors his new love offers in a theater. Then, later, she brazenly poses the question every dumpee wants to ask her dumper: "Are you thinking of me when you fuck her?"

Once again, she was using a real-life situation to inspire her art. After finally speaking to an ex-boyfriend a year after their breakup, she realized she was still disturbed by the split because, "I thought, 'God, a year has gone by.' I guess I was hoping that during that year I had consciously begun to move on." She hadn't, so she began to "write down everything that I was feeling, just so I could get down to exactly what I felt."

The hard-driving melody and Alanis's powerful vocals gave the song a sense of excitement and energy that was hard to resist, but it was the in-your-face, to-hell-with-being-polite lyrics that really gave the song its edge. While the language and subject matter might seem shocking and rude on a first listen, though, neither was intended as a gimmick to grab some quick attention. Rather, it was simply an uncensored outburst from someone not afraid to speak her mind, an injured soul still struggling to find her self-esteem. Most people might want to keep these thoughts to themselves, but Alanis couldn't repress her feelings any longer.

"A few lines in there had me thinking, 'God, this is exactly how I feel, but I don't want to hurt anybody,' " she would later remember. "For years I had been a little guarded, but that was horribly unfulfilling. Glen said to me, 'Just remember how bad you felt when you did censor yourself. You have to do this.' So 'Are you thinking of me when you fuck her' was 100 percent honest. . . . It took me about a day to get over it, to let go of the fear of how it was going to be responded to."

All Ballard could do was sit back and let his cowriter and confidante work out her feelings through her music. No matter how emotionally naked it left her feeling. "Maybe she did think, 'Oh my God!' but I was there to say, 'That's really you, that's what it should be and it's beautiful,' " Ballard has explained. "When she stood behind that microphone, it was obviously coming from such a deep place within her. There are few more intimate moments. I couldn't imagine anything being more precious to her so I had a religious intensity about getting it right."

It's easy to get her meaning wrong, though. There is so much anger in both Alanis's words and her voice, it's easy to assume the tune is some sort of revenge fantasy. Male-bashing you can mosh to. As you listen to it, you can't help but wonder, "Who is the guy that can inspire this kind of rage, and what body part would she rip off first if they were ever to meet again?" That debate would certainly take place in the press as her record began its climb to the top of the charts. Still, Alanis would insist repeatedly that the goal in writing the song was not to get even. It was simply to get mad, at herself as much as the guy in question.

"If it was written for revenge, I think I'd be telling everyone his name. . . . I'm secretly grateful to him for walking away from a relationship that wasn't very healthy," she would explain to one interviewer. By writing "You Oughta Know," she was able to recognize and then dispatch with her own jealousy. It became apparent to her later that during the ill-fated fling, she "didn't have enough self-esteem to know that perhaps sometimes people break up because of incompatibility. At the time, I took the breakup as a slight. But I'm happy to say that now I'm no longer at a point where I put my self-esteem in anyone else's hands."

With each song she and Ballard worked on, she was able to learn a little more about herself. Suddenly, her music wasn't just a way to make a living. It had become her way of life. She had a sense of purpose, something that had been lacking in her early days as a singer. It's not like she disavowed any knowledge of her days as Canada's favorite disco teen, but she was at least now able to put her past in the proper perspective. She had been "writing for the sake of entertainment," Alanis told an interviewer. "I was using my voice as an instrument as opposed to a way of communicating. So I wasn't willing to write about the whole transcendence of pain I had experienced as a teenager."

It wasn't just Ballard that helped her delve deeper into herself in order to discover who she was and what she had to say. It was also her new hometown. Los Angeles had "helped me become angrier," she would admit in an interview shortly after the release of *Jagged Little Pill*. "It's helped me realize it's okay to be a little cynical, and it's okay to be assertive at the temporary expense of someone else in order to keep your self-respect. . . . There's a lot of darkness here, but it's also made me stronger."

Such comments were no doubt inspired by an incident that occurred not long after she had moved to Southern California. Alanis was living temporarily in a friend's home in Hollywood, when she was mugged in her driveway. She had just come back from working out, and was on her way to Ballard's studio, when a couple of guys suddenly appeared. They took nearly everything she was carrying and forced her to lie on the ground alongside her car. Lucky for her, the one thing the thieves didn't abscond with was the book of lyrics she was carrying.

If not for that stroke of luck, there might not have been a *Jagged Little Pill*, at least not in the form people would come to know it. The incident would be stressful for anyone, but it had to be even harder on someone who had just moved into this new city. Alanis didn't dwell on the incident when she arrived for work at Ballard's home, but it was apparent it had been a traumatic experience. Even several weeks later, while she was visiting in Toronto, she had a hard time shaking off the incident.

Arlene Bishop, her friend from the Song Works days, happened to run into her at a party, and it wasn't long before the conversation turned to the crime. "She was bummed out about the mugging," Bishop remembers. "She was shocked, and disappointed in humankind. There was a gun involved. There was fear involved."

After Alanis had given her former writing partner the whole story, Bishop tried to kid around with her. Pretending her hand was a gun, she feigned robbing Alanis, who put up a good front by laughing at the gag. "She said, 'Don't ever do that again,' and laughed again," says Bishop.

She kept up this good humor when hanging around friends, but in those quiet moments when it was just Alanis alone with her thoughts, it was a different story. Maybe it was her longing to break away from her old image. Perhaps it was the tension of trying to reconcile the fact that she was at once a very sexual person and a good white Catholic girl. It could have been the mugging setting off fears about her move to the strange, self-absorbed city of Los Angeles. Certainly being far away from the family she had long been so close to, who had always been there when she needed someone to lean on, didn't help. Whatever the reason, she began to experience what she would later describe as break-downs. She was learning how to channel her hopes and fears into music, but outside of Ballard's studio, life was not so easy to struggle through.

The problem, she would later theorize, came from being passive-aggressive. Ever since she'd started singing, she had worked with older people who sought control over her and her career, she figured. They constantly advised her on how she should conduct herself, and although she resented this, she politely took their advice and did as she was told.

Now, though, she was on her own and in charge of her life. Which can be pretty frightening when you never developed the emotional tools necessary to keep in control. Her feelings of confusion finally came to a head during the Christmas season of 1994, on a flight back home to Ottawa. She was writing her "fifty-sixth Christmas card on the plane when I had a head-on anxiety attack," she has explained. "I just bawled my eyes out and started shaking and wanted to faint. It scared the living shit out of me."

The crying and the fainting didn't go away, and Alanis

checked herself into a hospital, finally realizing that she needed to get some help. It came in the form of therapy, which she went to even as she and Ballard were still piecing together *Jagged Little Pill.* It was, for lack of a better word, ironic. The songs were therapeutic kernels of wisdom for her fans, but their author was still looking for something to support her when it came to coping with her life.

Therapy could teach her to release the negative feelings that had built up inside her, but only through her music could she truly let them go. No wonder she continued to work so hard with Ballard, continued to go back into the studio along with a variety of other musicians, in order to juice up the spare demo tapes with some more energetic, electric sounds. The songs were her salvation.

Some songs didn't need any extra muscle, like "Hand in My Pocket," which was always intended to be just Alanis on harmonica and Ballard on guitar and keyboards. Others, however, got a serious kick from special guest stars. After hearing an early recording of "You Oughta Know," Red Hot Chili Peppers' bassist, Flea, and guitarist, Dave Navarro, "asked if they could try something with it," Alanis has said. "I love them, so of course, we were all like, 'Yeah, of course.' I mean, why wouldn't you want them to play on your record, your song?"

Another big name who liked what he'd heard of Alanis's work and pitched in was Benmont Tench, accomplished keyboardist and member of Tom Petty and the Heartbreakers, who showed up to work on not only "You Oughta Know" but also "Right Through You," "Forgiven," "You Learn," and "Mary Jane."

It was exciting for her to watch her record being pieced together, to hear these little segments of her soul really start coming to life. Exciting, and stressful. Her manager, Scott Welch, found her a personal trainer, which let her work out any tension the recording process built up while also getting her fit for a long concert tour that would coincide with the upcoming release of her new CD.

Dave Matsorakis noticed early on that his client was susceptible to stress. "At one point, she had a lot of acne," says the trainer, whose other clients had included everyone from Leonard Nimoy to Jane Fonda. "She told me the doctor told her it was because of the stress. But then, there were other times she'd stare and then just start laughing. I'd ask her what was going on and she'd just say, 'Everything is going so great.' "

That might have been a bit of an overstatement on her part. After all, she was unable to pay Matsorakis for the training sessions she took every Monday, Wednesday, and Friday at ten A.M. He took her on as a client primarily because he had a good working relationship with her manager, but after three or four workouts, he really began to like Alanis and didn't mind getting a delayed paycheck. When she came to him a month after she'd started and said, "I'm taking too much of your time," he told her not to worry. They were having so much fun together, perhaps he should be paying *her*.

Even though Alanis was showing up at a Santa Monica athletic club after recording sessions that lasted until 3 A.M., she was never without a healthy reserve of spirit and energy. Matsorakis would put her through a rigorous round of weight-training, a full-body workout using fourteen different machines. That was usually followed by three- or four-minute intense sessions on the treadmill, which Alanis would get through with relative ease. At least she always had enough left to laugh it up with Matsorakis.

"People would come up to us and say, 'Are you working out or are you just playing around?' " says the trainer. "I'll never forget her laughter. There was no negativism about her at all."

He was so taken with Alanis, who had only recently settled into a modest apartment in Santa Monica not far from the gym, he invited her to his Super Bowl party after little more than a week of training her. And even though she sat in the corner "as quiet as a mouse," Matsorakis recalls, her subdued charm still managed to win over whomever she did speak to.

"She was absolutely the nicest person," recalls Carol Bivans, an actress and fellow Matsorakis client. "You wouldn't have known she had that big voice."

One topic she didn't mind talking about at the party or in the gym during the weeks to come was the progress she was making on her record. It wasn't that she was bragging. Rather, she simply "wanted to talk about how it was working out," says Bivans. Back in Canada, she was similarly confident yet low-key. During one trip back to Toronto, she bumped into her friend and former cowriter Bishop at a gym and as the two were stretching out after an aerobics class, they talked about their respective works-in-progress.

Alanis was very supportive of her pal, pressing Bishop for details about the record she was working on. When Bishop turned the tables to ask Alanis about her record, though, she tried to downplay the results. "I don't know. We'll see how it works out" was all she said about the subject.

Such modesty couldn't fool Matsorakis. As spring rolled around, he sensed Alanis's quiet confidence, although he still couldn't figure out her music. "Are you like Celine Dion or Madonna?" he would ask her. Finally, she brought in a tape with early mixes of *Jagged Little Pill* in order to fill him in. He knew even before putting it on that this was something special; he took it home and told his wife as he started to play it, "Sit down. This is our future."

No doubt he was talking about Alanis as a client who, even though she would not pay for her sessions until a couple of months later, might become popular enough to become his next Jane Fonda. However, his words were far more prophetic than he could possibly have known. The tape he was listening to was the near-final version of *Jagged Little Pill*, and it represented the future not only for Matsorakis but for all of rock and roll. All Alanis and Ballard needed now in order for the world to know about their work was that the record label they had signed on with would get the word out about exactly what she was up to.

Six

In a sense, Guy Oseary was to the business half of the music business what Alanis Morissette had been to the artistic end—a young go-getter who had achieved far more than a mere mortal was supposed to before even being old enough to take a legal drink.

At the age of twenty-two, he was already working as an A&R executive, responsible for acquiring and developing talent, at Maverick Records in Los Angeles. The Israeli native who moved to the United States when he was six had been an overachiever from his earliest days. Growing up in the mid-1980s as a fan of bands like Culture Club and the Smiths, he became adept at scoring free rides to the shows from other fans, and coming up with free tickets once he got there.

After enrolling in Beverly Hills High, Oseary also proved adept at getting to know fellow students whose parents had jobs in the entertainment industry. That led to a meeting with Freddy DeMann, who had once comanaged Michael Jackson and was now more concerned with handling his primary client, Madonna. Oseary had already become a bit of a minimogul himself, getting to know rapper Ice-T and receiving demonstration tapes from young rappers eager to find a record deal. He took one of these tapes to DeMann, who was impressed with both the music and the man pushing it, and suggested Oseary keep in contact.

Flash-forward two years. As part of her new recording deal with Warner Brothers Records, Madonna is given her own label, Maverick Records. When it comes time to look for someone to do A&R work, DeMann remembers the eager young guy from Beverly Hills High who is now attending a local college, managing rap groups. Within a couple of years, his signing of Seattle grunge group Candlebox became Maverick's first big success story, with the band's self-titled debut disc selling 3.5 million copies.

He was hot, and he was only going to get much hotter. In late summer of 1994, he got a call from his attorney, who asked if he would take time out to meet with a female singer just about his age who was searching for a label deal. There was really nothing to lose by taking the meeting, so Oseary made time in his schedule for Alanis and Ballard.

Though it was too early to get discouraged, Alanis wasn't particularly enjoying the hunt for a company that would not only release her music but also understand it. She had sent her demo tape to about half a dozen labels, including Atlantic Records, but nothing seemed to be clicking. There was interest in her, but no bidding war. Considering the success her record would go on to have, it's hard in retrospect to understand why anyone would have passed on it, but there was one obvious explanation.

"The thing to remember was that it was male record executives listening to the tape," says Larry LeBlanc, Canadian editor for *Billboard* magazine, an industry trade journal. "They just figured it would never get played on the radio."

This was a time when labels were still scrambling to find the next grunge superstars, and didn't have time for anything else. "She was a hard-sell at the time," says one industry insider. "It was before the whole female-oriented pop thing started happening. It wasn't a trend. It was new and different. She was a young woman with a point of view

that was beyond the scope of those jaded executives looking for the next Nirvana.''

That would account for the rude treatment Alanis got at
one particular label. She and Ballard had met with the company's main talent scout, who had flipped for her music
and wanted to sign her. He took her tape and an eight-by-
ten of Alanis in her disco days into a conference room,
where a dozen men gathered around a conference room
table while ''You Oughta Know'' played over the sound
system. The scout passed her picture around, as the label's
chief executive asked out loud, ''Should I like this?''

As the talent scout gave a weak pitch on Alanis's behalf,
essentially saying, ''Here's somebody who has been
shopped to us. We can get her,'' the photo came to one of
the company honchos, who happened to be ogling a *Playboy* at the time. He removed the magazine's centerfold and
passed it around instead of Alanis's picture, and the sound
of snickering grew louder.

''This is awesome!'' joked one of the guys as he stared
at the Playmate. ''Look at those tits!''

When the laughter finally died down, the label boss ren-
dered his verdict. ''I'm not going to sign some aging disco
queen!'' he told the room. And that was that. Nobody had
bothered to really listen to the music. They knew about
Alanis's past, and didn't care to look into her future.

It was as if all the work she'd put into improving her
life, and thus her songwriting, was for naught. She was
right back where she started, with a bunch of older guys
trying to fit her into their idea of what popular music should
be. All that mattered was how well a disc could do on the
charts. And in fairness to the executives who were passing
on her, the demo tape they were listening to didn't sound
much like what the finished product would be. It was just
a rough mix of Alanis and Ballard performing, and of the
dozen songs on it, not even half would make it onto *Jagged
Little Pill*. The rest were mainly leftovers from her writing
days in Toronto, with titles like ''Bottom Line,'' ''No Av-
alon,'' and ''Used to Run.''

These songs were not as electric, nor as personal, as the

ones she was still busy crafting with Ballard's help.

"A lot of the songs were about 'she,' while the ones that ended up on her album were more 'I,' " says Cameron Carpenter, then MCA's A&R honcho. "I think she got less guarded about her music as she went along."

Alanis knew where she was heading. She was beginning to realize what she was capable of, and what her album could be if only a label would take a chance on her. Unfortunately, nobody seemed willing to take the time to really listen to what she had to say.

It was a difficult time for her. From the time she started singing professionally, she had worked with people she felt were more consumed with making a profit than making a meaningful record. This time around, Alanis was determined to prove her music wasn't about making money. When she would be told altering a lyric would increase a song's commercial appeal, she had to explain that she hadn't written the tune so "the kids will respond more." She'd written this material for herself, and if others related to it, that was a bonus.

She had resigned herself to signing with "the lesser of all evils" until she and Ballard wandered into Maverick headquarters. She sat down and watched as Oseary popped her demo tape into a cassette player, and waited for his reaction. It came almost instantly. Oseary tried to contain his excitement as he listened to "Perfect," but Alanis could sense that she'd finally found someone who got what she had worked so hard to say. She was impressed by how focused he was on her music, and appreciated the way the meeting went. It was, as she would later recall, "quick, no bullshit, 'Have a nice day, I'll talk to you later.' And he did."

Oseary may have attempted to downplay his excitement around Alanis, but he was another story altogether with DeMann. He quickly rushed across the hall to share his discovery of the Next Big Thing. "When I heard 'Perfect,' I flipped out," Oseary later recalled. "I immediately knew this girl had something incredible. I only heard one song but that song made me crazy. It was so powerful. I was, like, 'Wow!' ''

As he listened to her tape, his coworkers wandered in to see what the commotion was about. They heard the vibrations through the walls and everyone—''any age, any race, the rap, the R&B guys, the alternative guys, the older executives,'' he has said—wandered in to ask, ''What is that?''

His enthusiasm was one giant step toward landing a deal, but it was not the final one. An audition was arranged at Ballard's studio, a sort of ''Alanis Unplugged'' for a handful of Maverick executives. With Ballard on acoustic guitar, Alanis sang for them. Then a track from the tape was cued up, and she entered the recording booth she was by now quite familiar with to belt out another number.

The Maverick people were impressed enough to get to work on a deal as soon as she finished her set. *Jagged Little Pill* had found a home. Even the big boss was pleased. Madonna was intrigued by what she later referred to as Alanis's ''honesty, her pain, her hopefulness.'' There was one artist in particular whom she couldn't help but think of when she listened to her label's latest addition.

''She reminds me of me when I started out: slightly awkward but extremely self-possessed and straightforward,'' Madonna told an interviewer a few months after the release of *Jagged Little Pill*. ''There's a sense of excitement and giddiness in the air around her—like anything's possible, and the sky's the limit.''

There was still some work to be done on the record, adding in overdubs, for instance. However, one giant hurdle had been passed, and the second phase of Alanis's career was starting to look pretty secure. Word began to circulate that she had been signed to Maverick, and the buzz began to build. In February 1995, LeBlanc wrote that Alanis was ''one of the top five Canadian artists to look for.''

''I knew she had a tremendous amount of ambition,'' LeBlanc says. ''I felt that with the Madonna tie-in, she had a good shot. The fact that she used to do those dance tracks didn't phase me. At worst, she'd get attention in Canada because of Maverick and Glen Ballard. I instantly knew that [her CD] would be a cut above what was coming from Canada at that time.''

Her future was starting to look pretty bright, but Alanis remained low-key about it all. She continued to work out with Matsorakis and play her demo tape for friends. In her downtime, she liked to paint, creating acrylic abstract art like the bright red, green, and yellow works she gave as a gift to her trainer.

Those who hung out with her had no idea this was a woman who had just concluded a major record deal. Her Santa Monica apartment was decorated very simply, with hundreds of candles melting all over and the rooms filled with colorful paintings she had done. When she went out, she cruised around in what one friend describes as ''this cheesy four-door sedan that looked like something your dad would buy you. It wasn't the sort of thing you'd expect a rock star to drive.''

Life during this period was quite a contrast from those now faraway days as a child star in Ottawa. Back then, it seemed like every moment was dominated by work. There were benefits and assemblies to sing at, demo tracks to lay down, a perfect appearance to keep up. Finally, with a record she was proud of ready to come out and a supportive label listening to what she had to say, life was different. She was in control of what she wanted to do, and that included taking time simply to live the normal existence of a nearly twenty-one-year-old woman in the multifaceted city of Los Angeles.

Adds her friend: ''When I met her, I didn't even know she was a singer. She was the most peaceful, nonthreatening person I'd ever met. She'd just stand there and talk to you. She was always very interested in chatting.''

While Alanis was busy going out for tacos with friends, sweating in the gym, or even singing with friends for spare change on a Santa Monica street, the wheels of the music industry had started to spin on her behalf. Her manager had hired one of the country's premiere music public relations firms, the Mitch Schneider Organization, whose clients

have included a vast spectrum of big names, from David
Bowie to Duran Duran to Dwight Yoakum. Then, advance
cassettes of *Jagged Little Pill* started going out to some of
the nation's rock critics in April. Instead of playing up her
experience in the music world, however, a decision had
apparently been made to be low-key about Alanis's past
life. It was doubtful many American critics would know
much about her past and, from her management's perspective, there really wasn't much of an up side in pointing it
out.

The choice would come back to haunt Alanis as her success grew and writers delved into her past. Some critics
began to see her as a prepackaged entity that had dabbled
in teen disco music when that was hot, and had now simply
turned her attention to the angry female singer/songwriter
trend that was growing in popularity due to the success of
artists like Courtney Love, Liz Phair, and Polly Jean Harvey. This debate would only heat up over the next year:
Was Alanis an inspiration for the slew of female artists that
had begun to dominate the charts, or simply an opportunist?

For the moment, however, Alanis's handlers felt there
was no reason to trust how the press would respond to the
idea that this original, previously unheard-of talent wasn't
so new or unknown. If they heard about her days as Canada's version of Debbie Gibson, writers might be more in-
clined to dismiss her new work without ever really giving
it a serious listen. They'd look at the press release, realize
she'd never recorded any serious rock and roll before and
move on to the next CD. Or, even worse, they might bring
up her past while doing an interview, which could put
Alanis on the defensive. Instead of coming across as a new,
original voice speaking from the heart to her generation,
she might seem more like a pop singer whose career fal
tered with one style of music so now she was moving on
to try another genre.

It didn't help her reputation when rumors began circu-
lating that Alanis's management and Maverick had somehow pressured MCA to pull her first two releases off the
market before they could circulate in the States. The story

wasn't quite correct—"Her records had stopped selling," according to LeBlanc, and it didn't make any sense for MCA to keep them available.

Alanis certainly didn't seem particularly ashamed of the work she had done while still a teenager. "I'm not scared people might hear those records," she would tell an interviewer a few months later. "I never did *Playboy* centerfolds. There's nothing I regret. Maybe people will just understand my lyrics now a little more if they hear those records. It validates this record." And then again, maybe they wouldn't.

So, the marketing machinery that would sell Alanis to the public was relatively invisible. The tapes arrived on writers' desks with little fanfare, along with the dozen or more others that writers get on a weekly basis. There was no fancy packaging to grab the eye, no elaborate parties to introduce the artist and her music, no pestering phone calls to see what the reaction to it had been. Instead, Alanis was sent on a whirlwind, worldwide promotional trip to plug her CD. Wherever Maverick's corporate parent, Warner Brothers, had an office, she would go to play and to promote.

"For a long time, she went wherever [her management and label] told her to go," says LeBlanc. "She had basically no previous performance experience. They kept her low-key because they had to."

Starting in early May and running through mid-June, Alanis stopped in Calgary, Chicago, Toronto, Atlanta, New York, Dallas, Washington, D.C., Hamburg, Amsterdam, Paris, and London to drum up support for her work. Maverick knew it had a potential hit on its hands so the company adopted "a very aggressive approach," company general manager Abbey Konowitch explained at the time. "We got her on the road to perform acoustically for all the branches. We got her out to radio and retail and kept it very grassroots."

Jagged Little Pill may have been 180 degrees different from *Alanis* or *Now Is the Time*, more personal and less commercial, but they did have at least one thing in com-

mon. They all had to be sold, and that meant getting Alanis
out there doing some live performances and the old grip-
and-grin with anyone who could help with the promotional
push. Maybe this very public, self-serving display seems at
odds with the whole essence of her CD, which is so intimate and confessional. Welcome to the music business,
where the unofficial philosophy often seems to be, "If a
tree falls in the forest and nobody is around to get the sound
added to radio station playlists and then go gold, did it
really happen?"

Perhaps this was a coincidence, but while Alanis was
busy on her promo tour, she got another big boost in the
form of an editorial/interview written by Timothy White,
editor of *Billboard* magazine, the unofficial bible of the
music industry. It was printed a month before *Jagged Little
Pill* was to be released, and White's piece extolled the vir-
tues of this young talent who openly discussed not only her
former life but also the stress it created in her young life.
The article became a coming-out party of sorts for her.
Every radio programmer or record store owner learned not
only about where Alanis Morissette came from but also
where she was going. Which was straight to the top, if
White's enthusiasm was to be believed.

Featuring the headline, "Music to My Ears, Morissette's
'Jagged' Self-Healing," the article praised Alanis for her
"often severe writing voice" that had "the crackling cer-
titude of someone who's long past vulnerability or impul-
sive confessionalism." She was remarkably open in her
conversation with White, discussing everything from her
days on *You Can't Do That on Television,* to her days with
MCA/Canada, to the time she had her "freak-out" in her
parents' living room. His story left the clear impression that
this was an artist with something to say, whetting every
reader's appetite since it would be another month until most
of them could hear the CD. Who needed a massive advertising blitz when you can get free promotion like this?

"They were trying to figure out an imaging campaign,
and they never did find one," says White. "None of what
happened to [the record] could have been orchestrated. This

Alanis, age 12, already looking like a pop diva. *Photo by Canapress Photo Service.*

One of Alanis's early supporters, Ottawa musician/police officer Dominic D'Arcy, brought her and twin brother, Wade, to perform at a local children's hospital. *Photo courtesy of Dominic D'Arcy.*

D'Arcy congratulates Alanis at her parents' Ottawa home shortly after she signed her deal with Maverick Records. *Photo courtesy of Dominic D'Arcy.*

Winning the 1992 Juno Award as Canada's most promising new female vocalist is a real scream for Alanis. *Photo by Canapress Photo Service (Bill Becker), for Juno Pictures.*

Comedian/actor Dave Coulier met Alanis at a hockey game, and the two ended up dating for about a year. Many speculated that he was the inspiration behind "You Oughta Know." *Photo by Celebrity Photo Agency.*

The soft-spoken, meditative writer/producer Glen Ballard was the perfect complement to Alanis's introspective writing style. It was this unique chemistry that made *Jagged Little Pill* a phenomenal success.

After an early performance for the Maverick Records brass, Alanis spends time with her new boss, Madonna. *Photo by Jeffrey Mayer.*

Life on the road during the early days wasn't exactly luxurious, as evidenced by this Minnesota hotel where the band (l-r: bassist Chris Chaney, drummer Taylor Hawkins, guitarist Nick Lashley, road manager Mark Holdom, and guitarist Jessie Tobias) stayed in July 1995.

Alanis and bandmate Nick Lashley share a musical moment during the Prince's Trust benefit.

Alanis's way of relaxing after more than a year and a half of touring included competing in a minitriathlon just outside Los Angeles in mid-1997. *Photo © by Nobby Parks/Online USA, Inc.*

Sharing the prestigious bill with such veteran rockers as The Who, Alanis performs at the 1996 Prince's Trust benefit concert in London's Hyde Park.

was a very important record generationally, for anyone between thirteen and twenty-five. They saw her as a woman talking about a generation that had been taken too lightly. She galvanized this audience. Alanis Morissette got very young people interested in rock and roll again. She was the beginning of them getting off the Internet and away from Game Boy.''

Of course, in America, she was working from a clean slate. As far as U.S. record buyers were concerned, she was a new, untainted voice speaking directly to them. It was a different story up in her homeland, however. Maverick reportedly sent a representative up north three months prior to *Jagged Little Pill*'s release in order to get the word out that this wasn't the same cute, cuddly Alanis record buyers were used to. In particular, the label met with MuchMusic, the only national music video outlet available. The channel had given a fair amount of attention to the young Alanis, at least until it turned lukewarm about her ''Real World'' video; if anything was going to introduce the older, more serious Alanis to the nation, MuchMusic was the place.

''If not for MuchMusic, it would have been harder to sell her,'' says LeBlanc. ''Her disco days hadn't been forgotten, and she was still on TV in reruns of *You Can't Do That on Television.* Maverick did ask MuchMusic to stop playing her old videos. And [later] Alanis did a lot of Q&A's on the channel.''

The most critical way to sell any album, though, is on the strength of a single. That first song from an album has to be powerful enough to get heard on the radio, and then lure those who listen to it into the stores to purchase the entire record. In the case of *Jagged Little Pill*, there was as little doubt as to which tune had the greatest impact. ''You Oughta Know'' was as fiery and energetic as rock music can get and, combined with Alanis's confessional (and off-color) lyrics, it seemed there was no way this track could miss.

Instead of trying to crack the Top 40 world, Alanis's former domain, Maverick took the track to alternative-rock radio. It proved to be a smart move, distancing her forever from her old performing persona and building credibility with the young, hip crowd that was most likely to buy albums and go to concerts. The plan was to start going for radio airplay on June 5, a week and a day before the CD was set to be released. However, in May, influential Los Angeles modern-rock station KROQ decided to jump on "You Oughta Know" early. (By coincidence, it was the same station that Oseary had grown up adoring.)

Lisa Worden, the station's music director, realized this was no ordinary record when three Maverick executives—including general manager Konowitch—arrived at her office to play the song for her and the rest of the staff. Usually, one promotional person was more than enough to push an album, so the presence of the label's big boys meant something was up.

"The company knew from the beginning they had a star," Worden has said. The sales pitch wasn't in vain. She heard exactly what Maverick had heard in Alanis, realizing that the song was "huge instantly." "You Oughta Know" went on the air the next day and KROQ listeners didn't wait to make their feelings known.

"The phone lines completely lit up," according to Worden. "So we played it again an hour later. The girls look up to her, and the guys just dig her. It's a good match for both sexes."

A week after its debut, it was the number-one song at the station. It quickly became not just a rock song but a phenomenon, with friends calling each other to talk about that tune where the angry woman really lays into the ingrate guy whom she used to go down on in a theater.

This was a period when the hottest thing going musically was Hootie and the Blowfish and their nonthreatening, middle-of-the-road rock debut, *Cracked Rear View*. They were *Forrest Gump* to Alanis's *Pulp Fiction*. Nobody in radio could have been too surprised, then, when each playing of "You Oughta Know" caused the request lines to start blinking like a Christmas tree.

Other stations quickly caught on to what KROQ had discovered. In Atlanta, modern rock outlet WNNX put the tune on and it quickly became the most requested tune in the station's three-year history.

"She's got a great touch with lyrics," program director Brian Phillips told a reporter, trying to explain the Alanis phenomenon. "It's very mature—she cuts right to the bone. She played here acoustically, and as we were watching we got the sense that she will be a force to be reckoned with. We all just thought, 'Wow, this is a moment we'll all remember.'"

In Boston, another of the country's most influential stations, WBCN, slipped "You Oughta Know" into the rotation and saw instantaneous results. A national promotions representative from Maverick had traveled to town with a test pressing of the single, a clear indication of how important breaking Alanis Morissette was to the company. That point was not lost on WBCN's program director, Oedipus, who needed no convincing by the time the song had finished playing.

"It was the attitude," he says, recalling the moment. "It was so nasty, filled with rebellious attitude, which is what rock and roll is all about. I was, like, 'Wow! I want this on the air now!' These types of artists are few and far between."

This was the kind of excitement a programmer lives for, but only occasionally gets to experience. For Oedipus, it was like the first time he ever heard the Clash. The music flew off the disc and slapped him in the face, demanding to be heard. A healthy number of Bostonians who heard "You Oughta Know" agreed. WBCN listeners, Oedipus happily recalls, fell all over themselves getting to the phone to request it again. And again. And again.

By mid-June, the track was already blowing past less-compelling competition, such as "I'll Be There for You," the Rembrandts' theme from the TV show *Friends*, on its way to the top of *Billboard*'s Modern Rock Top 30 chart. More amazing, though, were the initial reports on the success it was enjoying in Canada. Warner Brothers claimed it was experiencing "an incredible response" to the song's first week on radio and on MuchMusic, and a new generation of young CD buyers who knew nothing of Alanis's previous work flocked to *Jagged Little Pill*.

While this was certainly true, that doesn't mean it was easy for Alanis to earn some respect back in her native land. Her label had readied itself for a backlash, going so far as to hand-deliver copies of *Jagged Little Pill* in unmarked cassette boxes to Canadian reviewers just in case the name alone might color what they wrote.

Alanis still had the reputation as "being this platinum-selling dance queen," says Rob Robson, music director at Vancouver, British Columbia, rock station CFOX-FM. And because "You Oughta Know" had "such a heavy drum machine sound, dance stations played it" initially. At the same time, because the song was much harsher musically and lyrically than what Canadians had come to expect from her, there were plenty of skeptics who weren't entirely sold on Alanis II: The Sequel.

Even her former Canadian label, MCA, had been put off by her shift in direction. Executives there had heard the demo tape and were offered a deal to distribute *Jagged Little Pill*. The music was passed around the office, but it was considered such a radical departure for Alanis that it was hard to believe anyone would buy it. "People were so thrown by it," according to Carpenter, that MCA decided against paying for Canadian distribution rights.

"She went away the prom queen and came back Sissy Spacek in *Carrie*," LeBlanc says of the initial perception of Alanis back home. "The reaction was, 'Whoa! Shocking!' But there was the question of whether or not [she] was credible, a question that still lingers. Often the people who think the worst of you are the ones where you're from."

Alanis sensed the apprehension when she did a handful of interviews with Canadian journalists. These sessions would occasionally turn into adversarial situations, with her trying to talk about her new music and the writers going back to her earlier work. "They'd tell me my records sucked and that what I'm doing now is contrived," she later explained. "If it was that calculated, I must be pretty darn smart. Don't give me that much credit."

The heat was particularly on back home in Ottawa, where radio stations said the record didn't fit their demographic and wouldn't play it. Local musicians argued about how much credit she should be given for all the success she was starting to achieve. If it was any consolation, at least some of her old friends and fellow musicians were able to recover from the initial shock of hearing the lyrics to "You Oughta Know" and learning to accept what she was trying to do.

It wasn't easy, especially since a lot of them hadn't seen her in a while. "When I first heard [the song], I thought, *'That* came out of the mouth of our sweet little girl?" said Geoffrey Darby, who had directed her back in the *You Can't Do That on Television* days.

Alan and Georgia moved front and center to support their daughter. Okay, so maybe the language and subject matter of her first post-disco hit weren't exactly the kind of thing kids normally say in front of their parents. That didn't matter. The Morissettes were not your normal parents. When asked what her folks thought of "You Oughta Know," Alanis simply explained that they would say, "No, she's been that way her whole life, she just wasn't doing it publicly. And we're glad she is now." She proudly recalled how her father had called her up after his first listen to her CD to tell her, "So you're expressing a lot of emotion. That's good."

Equally supportive was her first mentor, Dominic D'Arcy, who still recalls being "taken aback a bit" after his first listen to her song. After that, though, "I went, 'That's Alanis!' A lot of people raised some eyebrows about it, but I knew differently. I thought, 'Good for you!' Many older folks said she's this, she's that, she's a slut, and I felt so hurt."

Her former English teacher, Bruce MacGregor, heard the same backlash when he was out and about in Ottawa. It hadn't been that long ago when he was introducing her to the volleyball tournament crowd as a future star and nobody was able to pick her out. The sudden success of *Jagged*

Little Pill had certainly changed that. MacGregor could sense that there was a contingent in Ottawa who had already seen and heard enough about their hometown heroine.

"They thought what she'd done was a sellout," he says. "I was so surprised. I think it was a radical change, but it was like the Beatles evolving. They started out doing Chuck Berry covers and then eventually started doing their own thing."

Of course, Alanis wasn't entirely on her own, since the disc was cowritten with Ballard, a guy who had been around for a long time and knew as well as anyone how to craft a catchy pop-rock melody. That left her open to charges that he was the one truly responsible for this burgeoning hit record, not her. Few who had written with her in the past bought this accusation. They knew Alanis too well. Maybe she'd been willing to sit back and let others tell her what to do when she was a teenager, but by the time she started working in Toronto, those days were over.

"When I worked with her, I never got the sense you could steer her in any direction she didn't want to go," recalls one of her old writing partners, Steve Haflidson. "I didn't sense it was Glen Ballard. It was Alanis speaking on the record. She'd worked with a hell of a lot of writers, and she knew when things were working for her."

The recording industry in Canada, which, according to LeBlanc, "thought she had come and gone," was caught off guard by the way in which the big-haired, well-tailored innocent who had disappeared from the charts not quite three years earlier had transformed herself into a goddess of grunginess. "I was surprised," says her former boss, MCA Canada president Ross Reynolds of the shift. "I hadn't fully anticipated that striking a transition."

If ever there was a time for a little gloating, this was it for Alanis. She had spent so much of her early life trying to be the happy, relentlessly positive kid in order to please everyone. Her days were spent worrying about how others were going to perceive her and her music, so she molded it to suit their needs instead of her own. So, now that she was putting her thoughts and feelings on a compact disc instead of tucking them away inside herself, and climbing up the charts as a result, she could easily have had the last laugh. She had certainly shown them what she was capable of.

Instead of mocking the reactions of those she had once tried so hard to accommodate, she sympathized with their concern. "I think my lyrics do scare some people, particularly those who knew me when I was younger," she explained shortly after her CD was released. "When they finally heard this more honest part of me, I think they were like, 'Yikes!' "

Their thoughts about her music didn't interest her nearly as much as those of the fans who were now starting to view her as their personal guru. As she sat down for a *Los Angeles Times* interview in July 1995, just as the record was really starting to break, she overheard two women talking at a nearby table. It was moments like this one that really let her observe the impact she was already having.

"One [woman] was talking about her boyfriend and she said, 'Yeah, that Alanis Morissette song really hits the nail on the head.' Gee, that's so weird," she told her interviewer. "I think for the most part, people are just happy to hear that I'm being honest. In a roundabout way, when I'm being vulnerable and honest, it's enabling them to be like that too."

This moment in the restaurant spoke volumes about exactly how different Alanis's life had become. During the days of her first records, she seemed eager for celebrity status. Making music was fun, but along with that came performing and doing appearances all over town until she was instantly recognizable. It wasn't just her music that was being sold. It was her positive personality, her exotic beauty, her youthful energy that were being peddled as well. With *Jagged Little Pill*, though, the emphasis had shifted. She had a Top 10 album in the United States but was able to sit right next to a pair of fans who didn't even notice her. It was the music that had made her marketable, not her image. Not yet, anyway.

This didn't happen by accident. The CD cover features

a pair of obscured shots of her face, offering only a partial glimpse of what Alanis looks like. Included inside with the lyrics is one other photo, but the shot is from the back and all you see is Alanis swinging her long, dark hair. The video shot for "You Oughta Know" took a similar approach, never offering up a full-on look at the singer. Instead, there are just grainy shots of her performing in Death Valley (where the video took three days to shoot), tossing her hair around and keeping her face hidden as much as possible.

This kept up the mystique that was slowly building around this unknown artist. Guys, in particular, were curious. Here was this woman singing about performing oral sex on her boyfriend in a movie theater, so what exactly did she look like? Alanis laughed about the fact that radio deejays wondered if she was "a dog or not," and made sure that nothing in the video was changed.

"The footage is a lot fuzzier than I thought it would be," she said when it began airing on MTV, "so when I saw that you couldn't really see me, I was like, 'We don't need to reshoot this, this is great.' "

She knew what she was doing. "You Oughta Know" wasn't a song about sex. It was a song about a woman trying to regain some dignity after a failed relationship. Still, there were plenty of young boys with bubbling hormones who might just focus on the R-rated material and ignore the emotions being vented. To them, the lyrics made Alanis sound easy. And if they learned how cute she was, Alanis might end up as rock's new sexpot instead of a legitimate artist.

The shock value of the song, whether intentional or not, was a double-edged sword. It made people pay attention to her music, but that left her open to plenty of misinterpretation. The most blatant instance of that came when she agreed to appear on KROQ's sex-oriented show, "Loveline," in which listeners call in with often-intimate problems and the show's host, a doctor, and the evening's special guest then offer some advice. The ribbing she received about her taking gentlemen out to movie theaters did not amuse her. Her trainer, Dave Matsorakis, saw her the next day and remembers that the way the hosts "kept harping on the sex part [of her song] . . . got her really pissed off."

It was time to move out of the low-key phase of *Jagged Little Pill*'s promotion and kick into high gear. The public had to get a look at her, see her in concert, to really be able to understand what she was all about. It was time to get serious. It was time to get out on the road with some musicians who weren't just in the business for the glory and the groupies. Alanis needed to find people who could not only play the music, but feel it as well.

Seven

*I*t was simply supposed to be a temporary gig. *Jagged Little Pill* had long since been recorded, but if Alanis was going to take her music to the people, she needed a band to back her up. There was no reason for any of the dozens of musicians who showed up at the cattle-call auditions to expect that they would be anything more than a hired gun brought in to help this up-and-coming singer do her star turn. Likewise, there was no reason for Alanis to assume something significant would click between her and any of these players.

The word was put out that this young singer was looking to put together a group to support her, and fifty people showed up to try out. For two days straight, she sang three songs with three different people every half-hour. Although she never came right out and asked any of the musicians if they understood what exactly she was singing about, that question was never far from her mind.

It wasn't that hard to find someone who could play flaw-less versions of her music. It was much more difficult to locate someone who recognized the art and the heart that went into writing it. If they didn't get excited about her work, it was difficult for her to get excited about them. For the first time, she was the one in charge of selecting a band whom she could tell what to do, after a lifetime spent as the person taking other's orders.

The first guitar player to try out was Jessie Tobias, who had grown up in Austin, Texas. He learned about music early in life, thanks to his father, who liked to play Santana and War records. It was in the sounds from the punk era of the late '70s and early '80s that he found music he could really relate to, and by the '90s, he was taken with the odd hybrid of punk, funk, and heavy metal styles popularized by Los Angeles–based groups such as Jane's Addiction and the Red Hot Chili Peppers.

While still in Texas, Tobias formed a band called Native Tongue, and in 1991 moved to Southern California in search of exposure and a record deal. He found both, but not much ever came of the latter. Refusing to get discouraged by this, he was able to work his way into vacancies in bands like Faith No More, LSD, and, best of all, the Chili Peppers. That was the good news. The bad news was he was let go from the latter group two months after joining it, and ended up working at a Malibu veterinarian's office, vaccinating dogs.

Like Alanis, he was struggling to find a place where he could be himself. "I felt like I didn't fit in," he later said of his Chili Pepper experience. "Right from our first photo shoot, I thought, 'This ain't me; it can't be.' "

At the Alanis audition, Tobias was paired up with the first drummer who tried out, Taylor Hawkins, who had played in several bands but was still looking for a place to establish himself. The two musicians locked in together very quickly, and less than a week after they came in, they were hired.

The next to sign on was bass player Chris Chaney, who would be the trained professional in the group. The San Francisco native had attended the prestigious Berklee College of Music in Boston, leaving when he was just a few credits shy of graduation, and was teaching bass and playing jobs around Los Angeles when he heard about the Alanis auditions.

The final piece of the puzzle was Nick Lashley, the only guy who didn't have to participate in the cattle-call tryouts. The tall, lanky Englishman was a rock veteran who had turned to music when a free-spirited uncle let him listen to the Beatles and Pink Floyd. As he got older, he grew to love the intricate, atmospheric guitar stylings of U2's The Edge and the Police's Andy Summers, something he put to good use in the 1980s with his band, King Swamp. After that, he backed up the Pretenders' Chrissie Hynde, and toured in a band backing another Canadian female rocker, Sass Jordan.

He had experience, but not too much experience. Exactly what Alanis was looking for. People who had been doing this for decades might be tired of the touring routine. Doing shows every night might become a job instead of an adventure, and the lack of enthusiasm would bring everyone down, from Alanis to the audience. So, finally satisfied with a youthful lineup (Lashley was the only member over thirty), the rehearsing began.

They may have started as little more than Alanis's backup group, but it didn't take long for Tobias, Chaney, Hawkins, and Lashley to notice that there was something different going on. They weren't just the boys in the band. They were partners.

"This whole thing started out as her thing and she's been so great in including us in things that most pickup bands or backing bands wouldn't get to do. She wants us to be a *band*," Chaney recalled later. Lashley also would observe that his new boss "encourages us to put our own personalities and our own creativity into the music, which isn't the case when you go on the road as a hired-gun kind of guitarist."

Alanis had one essential rule for them to follow, and after that they were on their own. "The whole idea behind *Jagged Little Pill* was that it was created spontaneously in the studio," she has said. "There's something to be said for just letting a song become what it wants to be in a live show."

She wanted her concerts to seem fresh and new—not

surprisingly, since the whole concept of touring was new to her. She hadn't done many full-scale live performances to promote her two dance-music albums, so the idea of preparing for a massive tour to support *Jagged Little Pill* was both challenging and daunting. A promotional road show that would involve some live gigs, along with the usual glad-handing visits to radio stations and record retailers, was set to coincide with the mid-June release of the album.

The plan was to bring Alanis and the band along slowly. Let them get used to each other and to the music. They'd start out performing at small clubs and concert halls for the first few months, build a fan base, and really come together as a group. Then it would be time to move up to larger venues. To prove they were ready for what would eventually become a year-and-a-half sojourn all over the globe, though, Alanis and company had to perform a couple of warm-up shows, first for Maverick and then for a real audience.

The Maverick show started out as a small affair. It was essentially just a way for Alanis and the new men in her life to practice in front of an audience. They'd really only had a crowd once, when roughly fifty to a hundred friends came to hear them play at a San Fernando Valley soundstage, and only a handful of people were expected to show up when she performed for the label executives. By the time Alanis stepped onstage for her first rock show with a real rock band, the crowd numbered close to three hundred. Plus one special guest.

"No pressure," Alanis joked later. "It was only Madonna."

The boss had shown up to see what her young charge had to offer. What she saw was a ferocious performance that caught at least some people who knew Alanis off guard. She seemed so reserved and polite away from the stage, but when she launched into her show, she became something else. A dynamo, a live wire, a woman on a mission.

"The only time I ever saw her different [from her usual

quiet demeanor] was when she got on that stage, and Madonna was there,'' recalls her trainer, Matsorakis. He remembers his client pushing herself so hard, by the end of the miniconcert he could see her gasping for air. Her physical conditioning needed a little work. Her music did not. The execs seemed pleased with the results and it was time to move on to the next phase. A real audience.

A couple of showcase performances were arranged at two small, very fashionable Los Angeles–area clubs, Luna Park and the Dragonfly, in late April. ''You Oughta Know'' was just beginning to get some airplay in town on KROQ, and the buzz on *Jagged Little Pill* was building to the point where it was more like a thundering roar. That gave the showcases more attention than Alanis or her management team may have wanted. Instead of simply being warm-up performances, the heat was on her to be at the top of her game.

''Now this twenty-year-old woman was under the pressure of a major showcase,'' Maverick general manager Abbey Konowitch said at that time. ''It looked like part of a master plan, but it wasn't.''

Both shows were packed with a mix of music fans who wanted to see what all the fuss was about and slick young record business guys, the sort who usually prefer to hang back at the bar and talk through any show they go to see. Hey, they didn't pay for their tickets, so they have no investment in paying attention.

By the end of Alanis's forty five-minute set at the Dragonfly, the only thing anyone in the club had to say was, ''More! More!'' ''I was really amazed,'' says Ann Glenn, a record company publicist who went to the show. ''I remember she had so much energy, we walked out saying, 'We need this CD now.' ''

The bulk of the crowd for this latest dress rehearsal worked in the industry, but when Alanis stepped onstage to begin the show, they all dropped their cool facade and hurried to crowd around the stage. They watched in awe as Alanis was up, prowling around the stage like nobody they'd seen before. "You didn't want to leave afterward," says Glenn.

Not everything about the showcase was perfect. Alanis worked her way through all the songs from *Jagged Little Pill*, flailing her long hair like a weapon and sweating up a storm in a dark outfit complete with see-through shirt over a tank top, but she never really seemed to make a solid personal connection to the audience. At times, she seemed to be so caught up in her agitated stage persona that she forgot there was even a crowd out there. To some, it might have looked like an act, as if she was playing the part of a tortured artist. To her, it was just a bad way of coping with the stress of performing her material in front of a bunch of adoring strangers.

"There was a while where I was briefly swept away by what I now call 'the bullshit,'" she has said of her first several shows. "My fear was manifesting a persona onstage that was over-the-top and urgent. In time, the urgency turned into a more relaxed and unapologetic expression."

In other words, she was feeling out the audiences as much as they were learning what she was about. Nervousness was understandable. These two performances marked the first time in her career she'd been able to do the kind of music she wanted to in front of a crowd who knew next to nothing about her or her career.

Alanis fully expected these gigs to be a bit rocky. "The earlier shows were truly all about me/us getting my/our bearings," she would say months later. "Trying to find the balance between entertainment and communication. I enjoyed the latter much more."

So did the people who came to see her. Before stepping onstage, in fact, she noticed that plenty of folks in the crowd were singing "You Oughta Know." Her album hadn't even been released. The song was playing on just one local station, and already people knew the words. Even at this beginning stage of the second phase of her career, she already had proof that she was connecting with people in a way she never had before.

This was the magic of live performance, something she

never really did back in Canada. Sure there were all those school assemblies and football games and promotional gigs, where she'd get up and do a song or two, but there was never really a time when she was allowed to do her music her way and truly connect with an audience. Now, after only a handful of shows, she was starting to feel downright religious about the experience.

"Being onstage allows me to tap into my spirituality," Alanis later said. "It's very difficult to be the spiritual person that I am—and that everyone in my band is—out on the road. But inevitably, every time we're onstage, that comes out. It actually becomes quite a self-indulgent process, being onstage. There's a lot of release involved, which is so needed when we're doing this."

She was ready. It was time. Alanis and the band packed their bags and hit the road, sticking with the game plan of hitting only the small venues. This would be a real no-frills tour, in anticipation of bigger and better things to come. "You Oughta Know" was starting to garner some attention and airplay, but if she couldn't demonstrate the same energy and attitude in front of a crowd, there was the danger she'd end up a one-hit wonder, just like in Canada, where she'd never developed any live performance skills. So, rather than fail in front of an arena-sized crowd, she'd work things out in front of a few hundred people in bars and clubs.

It was the Kmart of rock tours, with everything kept as affordable and basic as possible. Monitors to allow the band members to check their sound onstage were virtually non existent, since there was little time or money to get good ones. To play in Chicago as part of an outdoor festival that drew some forty thousand people, by far the largest crowd she had yet played for, she and her group found a cheap flight there and then headed out from that show to gigs in Minneapolis and Milwaukee in a rented Ford Econovan with their gear tossed into the back. Within two weeks on the road, the van floor was a burial ground for a variety of chicken bones, mashed melon pieces, and banana peels. The accommodations were similarly unspectacular. While in Minneapolis, the band holed up at the Gopher Campus Motor Inn, which came complete with a giant replica of a critter that looked a lot like Rocky the Squirrel out front.

Sometimes, the star of a tour will stay at the nicest hotel available, while the band gets stuck back at some Motel 6 alongside a railroad track. That's the name of the game. If your name is on all the T-shirts and programs for sale at the show, you're the one who gets the deluxe treatment. Alanis, however, acted like anything but a star. No matter how bad a place was, there was still no separation in status between Alanis and her band. She always got a separate room, while the guys had to double up, but that's because she was the lone female in this little family.

Sometimes, they didn't even have to worry about where to stay. They would go onstage at nine P.M. and then head out in the van for the next gig in the wee hours of the next morning. Along with various tour managers and roadies, the crew would drive into the night, everyone taking a turn behind the wheel while the others slept. Alanis may have been the star attraction, but even she gamely volunteered to drive. The unlucky person who drove was often victimized by the running joke, one that would become extremely old by the end of the tour, of everyone else repeatedly asking, "Are we there yet? Are we there yet?"

Immediately after a show, that chant would be replaced with another: "Where's the tape?" Everyone wanted to listen to the recording of that night's performance as they drove, critiquing everything down to the last note. With every tape, though, there was a growing sense that this singer and her group were really coming together. Their sound was still a bit rough, but that's just the way Alanis wanted it. The record wasn't particularly smooth or slick, so the live show couldn't be either.

The crowds were responding in ways Alanis hadn't anticipated when she started work in Ballard's studio barely a year before, with only one set of eyes on her. By the time she got to Minneapolis, "You Oughta Know" was climbing the modern-rock charts, and the audience at that show responded more enthusiastically than she had ever expected. The people started thrashing around wildly, shocking the woman who was inspiring the moves.

"There was a mosh pit . . . when we played there," she later recalled. "Is it me, or is this music not about mosh-pitting?"

Maybe not moshing, but these were certainly tunes that promoted the release of whatever negative emotions you kept inside. Slamming into fellow concert-goers was certainly one way of doing that. More than this physical reaction to her music, it was the emotional reaction that seemed to affect Alanis. It was clear that people were appreciating and understanding what she had to say, but she wasn't necessarily certain that was a good thing.

"The reaction of the audience has been so amazing and open," she told a reporter during the tour's first few months. "It's comforting and bittersweet to know that I'm not the only one who's gone through these things. At the same time it's a little disturbing that apparently there's a lot of people out there having gone through such painful things. The reaction has been pretty intense."

Seeing that reaction from her vantage point onstage was enough for her. She didn't want to be one of those artists who constantly keeps an eye on the charts, judging success by how well their work is selling. "In many ways, it's better for me to be ignorant," she explained at the time. "I don't need to know if I'm climbing up the charts. I really just do what I feel. The good thing about the response, though, is that I don't have to feel alone in what I think."

Had she checked the charts, she would have seen she had plenty of company. On July 1, *Jagged Little Pill* entered the *Billboard* Top 200 at 117 stuck just below Gloria Estefan's *Hold Me, Thrill Me, Kiss Me* and just above a disc that had come out when she was still singing disco in Canada, Nirvana's *Nevermind*. However, just five weeks later, her CD had leapt into the Top 10. By the beginning of September, just nine weeks after its release, it had gone all the way to number three, within striking distance of the number-one record by another American debut, Hootie and the Blowfish's *Cracked Rear View*.

Tens of thousands of people were buying the record every week, but only a handful were able to see Alanis perform the songs live. Even when Sinead O'Connor dropped out of the summer's big Lollapalooza tour and Alanis was approached about taking her place, her management opted to keep her playing the small venues. Why mess with a plan that was working so perfectly? Instead of coming off as someone trying to capitalize quickly on her success, opening her up to charges that she was selling out, she seemed to be someone intent on keeping her music as personal and intimate as possible by sticking with small club shows. In her case, the line between artist and audience had been virtually erased.

Things didn't always go smoothly. Early on in the tour, Alanis would get so excited during a good show, with the crowd cheering and singing along, that she'd try playing acoustic guitar. Unfortunately for her, her playing was "what you'd say was best kept for a private place," according to one attendee at one of her first shows. It was hard to tell exactly what she was playing, because as a sort of mercy killing, the road crew would turn off her sound.

In Seattle, the tiny venue was so crowded Alanis and her band were unable to walk through the place and onto the stage; instead they had to go outside and then enter through a back door. In Vancouver, they played across the street from where guitar whiz Charlie Sexton was performing, and could only draw about three hundred people inside for their show, which included the sound system blowing out. And in San Diego, Alanis walked into a CD store for a promotional performance and instead of finding one of her CDs on display, she found three. The store had managed to locate her two Canadian discs. Up to that point, her old music had been pretty much left out of it. She didn't bring it up in conversation, so not many retailers and interviewers knew about it. Seeing *Alanis* and *Now Is the Time* may have been a bit of a surprise, and although she didn't remark on their sudden appearance, she did have what one observer called a "that's not what I expected to find here" expression pass across her face.

This wasn't the only time she was confronted by her past. Word had gotten around about her past life, and interviewers were starting to bring the subject up. When the tour eventually hit New York one day in mid-August, Alanis made the radio station rounds to promote her album and her show at a local club, Tramps, and the deejays seemed to particularly enjoy kidding around about it.

"It's like an illegal import," joked one jock. "It's like you can't get Cuban cigars and you cannot get Alanis Morissette albums in America."

"Right," Alanis shot back. "They both have the same effect on you."

She didn't seem to mind the mild ribbing about her old days. Within minutes, she had turned the tables on the deejay, conducting her own light-hearted interview with one of his coworkers, who she wanted to make sure was being treated with proper respect at the station. As it always did, conversation turned quickly back to *Jagged Little Pill* and the Canadian years went right back to being a distant memory.

Despite the occasional rocky moment, this first road trip produced nothing but smiles all the way around. Of course, the grinning might have been at least partially due to a contest Alanis and the band had initiated, one that didn't have much to do with music. Despite their hectic schedule, there was still time left in the evenings for some fooling around, so that became a game. The winner in this competition was the one who had slept with the most people by the end of the tour's first leg. (The winner was Jessie, with Alanis reportedly coming in third, and the one married member, Nick, exempt from playing.)

She may not have won the competition, but Alanis seemed to enjoy this new sport. "You Oughta Know" had given her a sexy reputation, so now it was time to live up to that. Call it Revenge of the Catholic Kid.

"I never allowed myself to go off the path when I was younger," she once explained. "There are a lot of things I didn't do. I lost my virginity at nineteen but I was very sexually active since I was fourteen, doing everything but.

Isn't that odd? I enjoyed what I was doing, but I couldn't fully enjoy it."

Now, at age twenty-one, it was a different story. She was enjoying every aspect of her sexuality. While conversing with friends in Los Angeles, for instance, she described incidents where she'd been hit on by lesbians. She seemed titillated enough by the experience that friends made her promise to notify them immediately if she kissed a woman while out on the road. (Unfortunately, she never reported back to the friend.)

It wasn't just the sex that was casual, either. So was just about everything else going on behind the scenes. Alanis had a few ground rules for herself—no smoking tobacco, no heavy drinking, no injecting or snorting of any kind— but she was a free spirit when it came to most other topics. Like clothing. She was fond of wearing thrift-store chic, dressing in such sartorial relics as polyester bell-bottoms, green suede tennis shoes, and oversized sparkly black shirts. Backstage and in interviews, she struck many as a refugee from the '60s, a hippie chick about twenty-eight years too late for the Summer of Love.

Clothing was so important to her, she took to selecting the wardrobe for her bandmates as well. They all had three different outfits they'd wear onstage, and Alanis took charge of deciding what they should change into. But it wasn't just clothes that made the band. As the tour moved along, she also became fond of painting the nails of anyone within finger's length of her. Gender didn't matter, nor did the color of polish. The members of her own band, the guys in the groups that opened for her, like Better than Ezra— they were all willing victims on whom Alanis slathered shades from black to robin's-egg blue to platinum (the latter coming as a gift from Maverick to celebrate *Jagged Little Pill* hitting one million in sales). The painted nails on her bandmates served two purposes. First, they made it clear that this was a group of guys willing to be as unconventional as the lady boss who wanted to put on the polish. And second, it was "a good excuse to get a guy to put his hand on your knee," Alanis liked to joke.

It couldn't have been easy being the only girl in this group of boys, even if she was nominally in charge, but she didn't seem to mind. In fact, she fit in rather well. It didn't hurt that, like most guys, she had a fondness for dirty jokes. "I have the filthiest mouth of them all. So I'm right there with the filth," she has explained. "I encourage it, as long as it's not derogatory."

Despite the ire and intensity that she had put to good use in *Jagged Little Pill,* there was another side to Alanis. This was one woman who in private could be funny, frivolous, and foul-mouthed. Maybe the public couldn't see this, but her band truly appreciated this ability to be just one of the guys.

"She can take a girl joke," Tobias once marveled, "but she also knows the difference between a pig and a guy who's having fun." At the same time, though, they also welcomed the more stable influence that came with having a woman in charge. They couldn't have a typical "guy tour," he added, sleeping with every groupie who showed up backstage. "Some of us guys need a little bit of that chaperone kind of thing."

The lines of communication between Alanis and these new men in her life were open twenty-four hours a day, with any problems being talked out right away instead of letting them sit and fester.

"Tell me what you're thinking," she would explain to them. "Even if it's something stupid, 'Alanis, I think the lights should be greener,' just come and tell me."

It wasn't always easy for the band. Everywhere they went, all the fuss was over their boss. Most pictures from concerts were of her. The interview requests were for her. The fans screamed for her. The limelight seldom shined on them, at least not to the extent that it bathed Alanis in its warm glow, but they never had the chance to work up any resentment. The boss just wouldn't allow it.

"If I feel like I'm getting dicked in any way, I can always go tell her exactly what's on my mind. We all can," Tobias explained during the tour. "And she really pays attention. Anytime we've come to her and said, 'Hey, we need a little more money,' or anything else, she's always listened."

All of this bonding that was going on off the stage inevitably started to be reflected onstage as well. The shows were getting tighter, the songs more focused than ever. Alanis was starting to feel more comfortable, slipping into her own little pre- and post-show rituals. Before each concert, she'd sip a cup of tea with honey and lemon to prepare her voice. To get mentally ready to sing, she'd slip off into her own world. There was no point in trying to carry on a conversation with her. She was lost in her private space.

After the concert, she would have to have ready a bottle of Bailey's and some coffee to unwind. That bottle was generally emptied by the next day, and there was one standing rule—nobody could drink from it until Alanis was done. Backstage following a show, she would also make it a point to meet and greet as many fans as she could. When it was time to go and she had to be led away by someone in her road crew, she would protest her departure and once gave one eager man the band's tour itinerary so he'd know where they were heading. (Of course, his constant phone calls after that encouraged Alanis to stop being quite so free with such information.)

It was the women she encountered that left more of a mark on her, though. As the tour rolled along, she became something of a patron saint to dumped and disaffected women. Tobias once remarked that the crowds were roughly 75 percent young females, and they all screamed along with every word that Alanis sang. Her music was the soundtrack to their lives, but she still refused to think of herself or her music as anything extraordinary. In fact, she figured it was the ordinariness of it that was striking such a chord.

"I guess it's a human sort of thing," she says of her fans' response. "The human condition is to feel. And if someone is expressing their feelings, I think that anyone can relate to it."

Her music may have been relatively anonymous, but her profile was certainly continuing to rise. As the summer of

1995 slowly turned to fall, Alanis was becoming a star on a level that far surpassed what she had experienced in Canada. When she returned home to Los Angeles for a sold-out two-night stand at the Ford Theater just up the street from the Hollywood Bowl, celebrity well-wishers like *Clueless* star Alicia Silverstone showed up backstage. All the newspapers, magazines, and talk shows were after her.

She went out of her way to avoid any media that could be construed as too mainstream for the young, hip, alternative image she represented. Her management team stuck to the original plan even as *Jagged Little Pill* sales far surpassed anything they'd ever dreamed of. They saw this as a CD that was speaking to the young and disaffected, and to allow Alanis to appear in something her fans' parents read might make her seem extremely uncool. Which in the music business can often be an unpardonable sin. So what if the Ballard-supplied pop hooks made the disc as purely catchy as anything in the Top 40?

"You have to give Guy Oseary credit," says one record label executive. "He was able to market and package Alanis right. *Jagged Little Pill* came off as an alternative record, even though it was just a pop record."

She picked and chose her interviews very deliberately. Every publication she appeared in had to be hip. Every TV show had to be cutting edge, at least compared to the alternatives. Alanis agreed to interviews with *Rolling Stone* and *Spin*, both of which put her on the cover in the same week, instead of *Entertainment Weekly* or *Us*. When it came time to do a late-night chat show, she performed on *The Late Show with David Letterman* instead of *The Tonight Show with Jay Leno,* daring to sing the F word in "You Oughta Know" even though she knew it would be bleeped out.

Alanis came across as an alternative rock star even as her CD continued to sell by the truckload. By the time she agreed to sing on *Saturday Night Live* in early fall 1995, she had achieved a goal that was unimaginable a year earlier. On October 7, *Jagged Little Pill* had surpassed the year's other surprise success story, Hootie and the Blowfish, to become the number-one record in the nation. Not quite three years removed from being relegated to one-hit-wonder status during some Canadian radio station's golden-oldie weekend, she had made it back to the top. Only this time, instead of her music making that climb by following in the footsteps of what was already popular, she had blazed her own trail.

Certainly it was a good feeling. It was vindication. It was revenge. Still, success was not trouble-free. Things had perhaps gone too well too quickly. That's the perfect recipe for backlash. Plenty of that resentment was already being served in generous portions back in her native country. She could feel it. After Alanis had finished a question-and-answer session at a Toronto radio station, her interviewer remarked that "some people can evolve, some people can change. Personally, I don't believe it."

This second time around for her career was going to be all about the work. It was the music that was supposed to matter, not the fame. She'd had enough of that once before, and while it was nice when she was up there winning her Juno Award and becoming the toast of Canada, the attention only made it harder for the public to take her seriously when she wanted to move in a new direction.

Still, she had the number-one record in America. Alanis Morissette was now officially a phenomenon, and her sudden rise to the top, along with the personal nature of her lyrics, had made her an object of curiosity. For music and social critics, it was now open season on her music and her life.

It hadn't been easy for her to get to the top. It was going to be just as tough to stay there.

Eight

*A*lanis never did get it. The whole idea escaped her completely.

The fact that there were all these people—men, most of the time—who made a living criticizing the life's work of musicians such as herself had long been totally alien to her.

"I think the whole concept of critics, whether it's about music or movies or anything . . . I just to this day still don't understand it," she once explained. "You know, commissioning someone to say whether they hate or love something. I don't know why people are interested in hearing another person's opinion."

This is usually the sort of complaint you hear from an artist who's endured one too many bad reviews, but the remark is more confusing coming from Alanis. That's because during the early days of *Jagged Little Pill*'s release, as "You Oughta Know" was just hitting radio, it was music critics who fanned the flames to give her career plenty of heat. At first, anyway, the reviews were almost always positive.

Early on, an influential music industry publication, the *Gavin Report*, set the tone for the gushing and raving that was to come. "There's no doubt that Alanis Morissette is on her way to becoming a big star."

It wasn't just the music press that recognized her abilities, though. Major mainstream publications were also weighing in. Under the headline, "You Oughta Know Her," *Newsweek* magazine's Jeff Giles first raved about that particular song. He referred to it as "a wonderfully fierce and sneering bit of pop that recalls Sinead O'Connor in her avenger mode." While giving Alanis and Ballard a mild slap on the wrist for having too many songs that "slide into bombastic power-pop choruses," Giles also singled out the CD's melodies and lyrics that "seem to float off the top of her head, as in fabulously carefree and shuffling tunes like 'Hand in My Pocket' and "You Learn.' "

USA Today didn't surrender much space to its review of *Jagged Little Pill,* lumping it together with a critique of another female singer/songwriter named Jennifer Trynin. Critic Anne Ayers kept it short and to the point. She gave the disc three out of four stars, writing that Alanis didn't just exemplify the angry-female-rocker craze. She transcended it, thanks to her "mature, assured songcraft and pointed writing."

Another glowing review came from a surprise place—Canada. Instead of burying this native sister, influential Toronto *Sun* critic John Sakamoto seemed to practically beam as he wrote about this "wholly remarkable" release. The complexity in songs like "Wake Up," he explained, lift *Jagged Little Pill* "far above a one-dimensional come-on and make it the most compelling coming-of-age album you're likely to hear all year." His review contained only one mention of Alanis's musical past, praising the power of her CD and expressing astonishment that "this is the same toothy performer who . . . cut a pair of innocuous dance albums in the early '90s."

Tom Moon, a writer for the extensive Knight-Ridder newspaper chain, seemed to take joy in Alanis's anger. Her music, he wrote, was "a strident distillation of old-fashioned singer-songwriter confession, full of anguish—but it's anguish with a purpose, communicated with serious lung power." Despite the rancor, he wrote that "these songs are never just bitch sessions. They turn on effortless, deceptively addictive melodies. . . . They elevate age-old rock-'n'-roll rebellion to a slightly more intellectual plane, utilizing a language that bounces between raw vitriol and the detached jargon of the therapy movement."

Her early live performances were also winning good notices. In San Francisco, *Chronicle* staff critic Michael Snyder gushed that Alanis had been "tremendous, spellbinding, wild" onstage. He pegged her style as a skillful blend of "confessional folk music" and "gutsy rock," and assured his readers that there was "no hype about it. Everyone ought to know about her, and everyone will."

Even the *New York Times*, in its own quiet and reserved way, seemed rather smitten with this young singer. Alanis's music was loud and uninhibited, precisely what the *Times* isn't, but critic Jon Pareles sounded rather impressed with her when he wrote that she sang with two different vocal styles. The first was that of a "good girl's mezzo-soprano, the voice of acquiescence and dutiful nurturing" while the second is a "pinched rasp on its way to a shriek; it's the enraged voice that appears when the good girl has taken all she can stand and starts to fight back."

One of the country's most serious newspapers was taking Alanis's music seriously. In mentioning her performance of "Hand in My Pocket," Pareles went so far as to call the song "an anthem that listeners can take to heart, as long as they're willing to raise their own voices now and then." This was one of the best indicators yet that Alanis's personal music was affecting more different kinds of people than she could ever have anticipated.

That was the good news. The bad news just took a little longer to get rolling. By the time *Jagged Little Pill* had leaped into the Top 10 and become an official overnight sensation, some writers had already become disenchanted with her. The *New York Daily News*, for instance, after seeing the same show witnessed by the *New York Times*, headlined its review, "She Does the Trite Thing," and ripped her for being the "latest and most transparent poster girl for female rage."

This negativity didn't exactly send her into a seething

frenzy. While they were filming a video for "Hand in My Pocket" the day after her concert, Nick Lashley cautioned her against reading the *Daily News* review and she shot right back that she had no interest in looking at either one; when a security cop asked her to autograph the piece, she wrote, "Don't believe everything you read."

The harsh words didn't stop there, though. In its year-end issue, *Rolling Stone* writer David Fricke wrote Alanis's music off as "more stylish argument than probing heart talk." He offered some faint praise for the "impressive bluster around the edges" in songs like "Right Through You," but griped that "too much sap runs in the middle" of her softer songs, like "Head over Feet" and "Ironic."

Meanwhile, *Entertainment Weekly* did have a couple of kind words for "You Oughta Know," but indicated that the rest of the album was "difficult to swallow." Critic David Browne griped that Ballard's arrangements were "clunky mixtures of alternative mood music and hammy arena rock," with Alanis "wildly oversing[ing] every other line."

He also criticized Alanis's lyrics, asserting that in her songs "men take her for granted and mentally abuse her, and she retaliates by threatening to leave one of her ex's' names off her album credits." In the end, he gave the CD a C+ grade, and the caption by her photo referred to her as "catchy and cranky Morissette." Such negative reviews didn't come frequently, but that sentiment was certainly out there.

As the summer of 1995 turned to fall and *Jagged Little Pill* turned into one of the year's most successful albums, the complaints about Alanis started to pile up. *Entertainment Weekly* didn't stop at a negative review. When her record hit number one, Browne took another shot with a story that was highly critical of Alanis's dance-diva days. He set up his piece by explaining right up front that her "seemingly overnight success is almost a textbook example of how to create a rock star."

Singling out her work on *Now Is the Time*, he explained that she was "vocally unrecognizable and could easily pass for Tiffany's Toronto cousin." As evidence that Alanis's life was more about being popular than being good, the article quoted one of her former mentors, MCA's John Alexander, who explained, "You knew she had a game plan. She has always done the right thing at the right time."

Browne spoke for a lot of critics when he cynically accused Alanis of tapping into "the anger thing." In particular, he saw *Jagged Little Pill*'s mix of musical styles—featuring everything from grungy guitar rock to freewheeling folk to power-ballad pop—as "if it were pieced together with the help of a focus group." Lyrically, meanwhile, his theory was that Alanis was simply trying to be all things to all people, serving up a catalog of personal grievances for everyone to relate to. Browne described it as "talk-radio pop."

The criticism was biting, but it wasn't exactly unique. This is the way it tends to go in the rock world. The problem wasn't that her music was unlistenable or her lyrics were too mundane. Rather, it was just the opposite. She had become successful, whereas other critical darlings had failed to catch on. That can be an unpardonable sin in rock and roll.

This was an era when Courtney Love and her band, Hole, were winning raves for their gutsy, grungy *Live Through This*, and Liz Phair's debut CD, the down-and-dirty *Exile in Guyland*, had music writers falling all over their thesauruses to find new ways to say "spectacular." Then along came a record capturing some of their rage, but also finding hope amidst the chaos of life and setting it to a catchier, radio-friendly beat (look no further than "Hand in My Pocket" for proof).

Alanis's and Ballard's past pop work may have been an asset when it came to creating tunes that would appeal to a mass audience, but to Browne and other critics, they were simply opportunists offering up a lightweight version of music pioneered by artists with more conviction to their craft.

"The album has the feeling of an emotional pep rally," complained Browne. "It's the dance queen Alanis after a few rough years in therapy."

There were other critical barbs. *Chicago Reader* writer Bill Wyman explained that "You Oughta Know" was "a vulgar piece of soft-porn attitudinizing" and "a riot of unoriginality." *USA Today*'s Edna Gunderson wrote that Alanis was simply "Tiffany having a tantrum" and seemed "whiny and insincere" in her lyrics.

Alanis's attitude toward the press didn't help. Just as her management team was determined to keep her from playing big concert venues, they had her avoid speaking to any major mainstream media. She would only do interviews with local newspapers and publications specializing in the music business. Nobody would be seeing her on a *Time* or *People* magazine cover anytime soon. *Entertainment Tonight* and Barbara Walters were going to have to wait. If she wanted to maintain any credibility with her audience, she had to be the reluctant star.

Thus, for most writers, trying to gain an audience with Alanis was only slightly less difficult than scheduling a breakfast meeting with the pope. The public relations firm representing her, the Mitch Schneider Organization, tried to be firm but fair. Requests for interviews were rejected with the suggestion that perhaps down the road, when Alanis's career was more established, she'd make herself more available. Even when she did speak to the sort of younger, more underground press, though, the interviewing process could be a bit tricky.

When Kim Taylor, a freelance journalist, first heard an advance copy of *Jagged Little Pill*, she immediately sensed there was something special about the woman who made it. She began trying to line up an interview for a now-defunct alternative music magazine she occasionally worked for. Five months and twenty-five phone calls later, she got it. And almost wished she hadn't.

When Taylor asked Alanis about entering "the second phase" of her career, the time when things might settle down after all the initial hype generated by the explosion of "You Oughta Know," Alanis explained that she didn't know what the writer meant. There were no phases. The next step for her "will be different, but just as exciting," she explained.

Taylor pressed the issue, though, pointing out that a lot of major media outlets wanted to talk to Alanis but were told to wait for that "second phase." The media reaction to that, she explained, was to take the approach *Entertainment Weekly*'s Browne had opted for and suggest that Alanis's career was being manufactured.

"I don't really even know what you mean by 'manufactured career,' " Alanis told her. "It's been a real organic thing for us. It hasn't been anything that we've all sort of sat around, put our heads together and thought of some marketing strategy."

Her priority, she continued, was her music and "not to talk to everyone who wants to talk to me. I'd want to talk to *Musician* before I talk to anyone else."

The interview was being done by phone and, Taylor recalls, there was so much static on the line that Alanis suggested she hang up and then call the singer's publicist. That way, the publicist could conference Alanis in and that would take care of the bad connection. Taylor complied, but was informed by the publicist that Alanis didn't want to continue the interview. It seems that their conversation had left her feeling both upset and offended.

A few hours later, Taylor received another phone call. This time it was someone in Scott Welch's office calling to tell her she was the first journalist to ever give Alanis attitude. Her questions about whether or not her career might be overmanaged were off-base. Alanis didn't speak to certain publications or TV shows because she believed they didn't reflect what she was about. Since she never read a mainstream magazine like *People* or watched a mainstream program like *Entertainment Tonight,* it seemed pointless to her to speak to them.

While appreciative of the artist's music, Taylor remained curious about Alanis's claims that she avoids reading any articles about her and never quizzes her manager about where the CD stands on the charts. "They really try to protect me from it so I don't have a breakdown," she had said. So, Taylor theorized, does that mean Alanis is simply a puppet for her label? She makes the music. They craft an image to suit it—in this case, the angry yet mysterious young female singer/songwriter—and hawk it like some new brand of jeans that all cool kids have to have. Taylor's questions remained unanswered. She never got to finish her Alanis interview.

Alanis knew being successful wouldn't be easy. She'd already been through it once. However, back then the knock against her was that her music was too shallow and superficial. For this second go-around, she was being chastised for being too open and honest, and that caught her by surprise.

"I laugh now. There were moments when I wasn't laughing," she has admitted. "If something's true, why are people so quick to doubt it? They've had the wool pulled over their eyes so often that they're compelled to throw the baby out with the bathwater, simply because they've been snowed so often."

She was smart enough to recognize that a lot of the griping came simply because she was popular. It's the same old story. When a CD started selling as well as hers was, that somehow implied it was without artistic merit. Hence, music critics were more likely to find fault with it.

"If this was a confessional record that I released independently and it didn't succeed, you'd believe it," Alanis would explain. "But because it's succeeding, you don't know whether to believe or not."

Her days as a pubescent pop star kept getting in the way. Even though few, if any, American critics had even known about her previous work, to those that had, everything they'd heard about her seemed quite a contrast to the Alanis they heard on *Jagged Little Pill*. It was hard to swallow the fact that anyone could change her persona that much in such a short amount of time, so many music writers remained skeptical of her success.

It wasn't just her image and music that got picked on, though. Her command of the English language also got raked over the coals because of the lyrics to "Ironic." The song offers up a litany of contrasting scenarios, like rain on your wedding day, a death-row pardon that comes just minutes too late, and a black fly swimming in your glass of white wine, and follows them up with one simple ques-

tion: "Isn't it ironic?" Some deejays and linguists wasted
no time pointing out that what she was describing was simply bad luck, not irony.

"What Alanis is singing about is a bunch of bummers,"
Duke University associate English professor Susan Willis
told a reporter. Irony, on the other hand, is defined by *Web-
ster's New World Dictionary* as an "expression in which
the intended meaning of the words is the opposite of their
usual sense."

The notion that criticism of her work had now turned to
a semantics discussion amused the singer. When the
"Ironic" question came up in an interview, she laughed it
off. "I guess what people forget is that when I write songs,
I write them sometimes in about twenty minutes. . . . It's
not something that I foresaw turning into a song, first of
all, that I'd have to sing every night for a year. Or something that I thought millions of people would be listening
to. Honestly, it was something that I just wrote as anyone
would write a poem."

In the midst of all the attacks on her image and her music, though, a few female writers began to notice a trend.
A healthy percentage of Alanis's detractors were male. In
a piece for the *San Francisco Chronicle,* Gina Arnold
mused that the singer may be the victim of a rock-and-roll
gender gap. The male-dominated rock press, she wrote,
loved to chide Alanis for her days as a young TV star and
for her disco discs and to speculate that Glen Ballard was
the real creative force behind *Jagged Little Pill.*

However, Arnold wrote, these complaints seemed rather
slight. Should she be banned from music for life because
of what she did as a teenager? Don't plenty of artists work
with professional songwriters? Perhaps male critics simply
felt uncomfortable with (and even a bit threatened by) the
thoughts she was addressing, particularly in "You Oughta
Know," which provided a focal point for every woman's
anger with the romantic vagaries of men. That's why they
saddled her with what could be perceived as thinly veiled
antifeminist buzzwords like "irrational," "hysterical,"
"spiteful," and "shrill."

Instead of burying Alanis for her forthright attitude, Arnold suggested critics praise her for trying to maintain as ordinary and uncomplicated a presence as possible. "She is certainly one of the few women singers to consistently appear in public in dumpy jeans, oversize shirts and bad hair," Arnold wrote, noting that this plain image created "a much more real form of feminine mystique. She exudes a sense of inner peace." In other words, this wasn't just some bitter woman bitching about a couple of bad relationships. Rather, Alanis was a maturing young soul who had learned to be comfortable with her own emotions, and was determined to convey this discovery to the world.

Even if "You Oughta Know" was just "a revenge fantasy that buys into men's idea of women having irrational meltdowns," as *USA Today*'s Gunderson described it, the song did seem to be about a woman who isn't afraid to express how she feels. To another female critic, the *Village Voice*'s Ann Powers, Alanis was at least exhibiting some energy and self-confidence and "if we're going to have a prepackaged angry-woman fantasy, better this than the ones we've had before."

Many discussions about Alanis's music tended to simply dwell on the anger and sexual content of "You Oughta Know," and how the two went together. Such debate was rather narrow, though, ignoring the issues and emotions raised by the other songs.

"People who are fans didn't see her as a woman rocker or an angry woman," says one of her earliest and most consistent supporters in the press, *Billboard* editor Timothy White. "She was an adult young person with an anger that had nothing to do with men. *Jagged Little Pill* sold fifteen million copies because young people were sufficiently angry about a lot of things. Her music was a young person's story, not just a young woman's story."

And so it went, for months. If nothing else, at least the Great Alanis Debate proved that her record was having an impact on people. Her previous albums were recorded, written about, and forgotten. Now, love her or hate her, people couldn't stop talking about her. And all the while, the sales for *Jagged Little Pill* just kept growing. By late October 1995, she had been bumped from the number-one position by Mariah Carey, whose slick, unconvincing blue-eyed soul album *Daydream* seemed to be the antithesis of all that Alanis was about.

Nonetheless, *Pill* set up camp in the Top 10 on the *Billboard* charts for the remainder of the year, dropping no further than number six around Christmastime when two other big guns, Garth Brooks's *Fresh Horses* and *The Beatles Anthology*, were released. Along with Hootie and the Blowfish, who were also still enjoying a long run of success with their American debut CD, Alanis had become a certified music industry phenomenon. She wasn't just selling people on her music. She was selling them on music in general.

"She was the anchor that kept the music industry going worldwide for about a twelve- to eighteen-month period," admits Canadian Recording Industry Association president Brian Robertson. "When you have one highly successful artist, that brings people into the stores to purchase other CDs."

Record sales had essentially flat-lined in 1995, thanks at least in part to albums that might sell well for a couple of weeks but burn themselves out too quickly and then slide quietly down to the bottom of the charts. This tendency to rush an artist into the marketplace with only a couple of killer songs in hand was a big problem for the industry, according to Michael Greene, president of the National Academy of Recording Arts and Sciences. And it was something *Jagged Little Pill* directly contradicted.

"She had one song after another, songs that took risks," Greene says admiringly. "The album was deep with new ways of exploring intelligent thoughts. Plus, her vocal stylings were so unique."

Meanwhile, she continued to tour virtually nonstop, both in the United States, the Far East, and Europe, and despite selling millions of CDs, Alanis continued to perform almost entirely in relatively small venues.

She'd moved up from clubs that could hold maybe one thousand people to three-thousand-seat arenas and civic centers, but considering the demand for her music, she could certainly have lured even more fans into bigger auditoriums if her management wanted her to go that route.

"We're trying to find a happy medium between turning thousands of people away and not having her play auditoriums," one of her management team, John De Hayes, told a trade publication at the time. The decision was based on music, not money. The smaller shows were a way of accentuating the power of Alanis's intimate lyrics and raw, unpolished stage show. She was connecting with audiences in a very personal way, and that could get lost if many in the crowd in a large arena could only catch a glimpse of her by gaping at a video screen alongside the stage.

"She understood why her record was a success—it's getting into a van and touring everywhere, making it an experimental thing," says *Billboard*'s Timothy White.

Of course, the strategy was also still allowing her to work out the kinks in her live show before exposing it to bigger crowds. It's not that the fans weren't enjoying what she was doing. In fact, they were completely enthralled with her every move, singing every word along with her as she stomped and whirled and shook her way across every stage she played. They'd even worked out a ritual for when she performed "Hand in My Pocket," high-fiving, flashing peace signs, and hailing taxis whenever the lyrics mentioned these activities.

However, despite all the energy she expended during her shows, there was still a sense that she was holding back a bit. Some artists, like Bruce Springsteen or U2's Bono, know how to work a crowd between songs as well as during them. They slip into engaging stage patter, telling stories and bonding with the crowd. Alanis, on the other hand, seldom chatted with her audience. After introducing her band, for instance, she would simply turn to the throng and ask, "And you are . . . ?" And that was it.

Not that any of this mattered to the faithful. She continued to sell out concerts, attracting a vast array of fans to her shows. There were the young Alanis-alikes with their long hair and dark clothes, rocker dudes, lesbian couples, hippie parents with kids, young married couples, and sixty-year-old guys all swaying and singing along with her songs. So what if she wasn't the most communicative person while onstage? She was speaking to them through her music. That was enough. And just what exactly was she saying?

"The truth," explained a trio of young females as they entered an Alanis performance in St. Paul, Minnesota, one night. Or, as *Billboard*'s White describes it, "the public expression of a personal truth."

Her critics would continue to disagree. To them, Alanis remained this cranky female singer filled with a rage that was at best misguided and at worse artificial. She was a product of an industry hunger to take the work of more legitimate women and water it down enough so that it would sell gobs and gobs of records. However, even if they were right, the issue had become moot by the beginning of 1996. Barely six months after her CD's release, she was no longer the plucky young Canadian trying to get comfortable with her life and her music. She was a bona fide, grade-A rock-and-roll superstar.

This wasn't just because millions of people were continuing to buy *Jagged Little Pill*. Popularity doesn't automatically mean an artist is going to leave his or her mark on society. Just ask Billy Ray Cyrus, Vanilla Ice, Hootie and the Blowfish, or any other new performers who suddenly burst onto the scene with a tremendous flourish, but are forgotten like yesterday's lunch once people discover there isn't much depth behind either them or their music.

Alanis was different. She had now become something more than just a musician with a hit record. Whether she wanted it or not, she had become a legitimate cultural and musical phenomenon. She had been anointed the unofficial spokesperson for her disaffected generation, and was also on the verge of becoming the most influential (and imitated) thing to hit the record business since the power ballad.

Nine

*I*f Alanis hadn't come along when she did, chances are somebody would have invented her anyway.

That's because just as *Jagged Little Pill* was being released, the time had become right for someone not only to take charge of popular music, but to speak for that group of disaffected teens and twenty-somethings known collectively as Generation X. They were supposed to be slackers, bored and ambitionless baby-boomer offspring who were growing up convinced that their futures were bleak. Life was never going to afford them the same breaks and good times their parents had, so why even bother trying?

There was just one problem with this reputation, however. Apparently, it wasn't entirely true. Movies like *Reality Bites* and *Slacker,* along with plenty of special TV news reports, gave the mistaken impression that this was one miserable age group, but that image didn't fit with the facts. A *Time* magazine survey found that contrary to the notion that Americans in their teens and twenties were pessimistic moochers, this was a very optimistic and self-sufficient generation, with 96 percent of the Gen Xers interviewed confident that "someday I will get to where I want to be in life" and 69 percent certain that they had to "take whatever I can get in this world because no one is going to give me anything." In addition, 91 percent agreed that "if I just work hard enough, I will eventually achieve what I want."

So, the slackers needed the world to cut them some slack. They actually did have hope and self-confidence, but it was hard to find anyone of this generation taking that message to the rest of the world. Kurt Cobain, lead singer/songwriter of the Seattle-based grunge band Nirvana, a band whose blisteringly angry, brooding guitar rock and bleak lyrical outlook on life was both compelling and incredibly depressing, had early on been anointed by fans and many in the media as spokesman for his generation. However, there were two problems with his receiving that title.

First, while Nirvana's music perfectly captured the life-sucks-and-then-you-have-to-probably-get-a-job-and-then-you-die attitude usually ascribed to Gen Xers, this didn't paint the entire picture of what the country's twenty-somethings were all about. Second, Cobain automatically forfeited his position as Gen X valedictorian when he killed himself with a shotgun blast to the head in the spring of 1994. He had taken his own lyrics about hopelessness and despair to the extreme, and that was pretty frightening. Being disaffected was one thing. Being dead was quite another. Slowly, the tide seemed to be turning. It was time for somebody else to step up, perhaps somebody with a more positive sound and message.

Music did change after his suicide, but at first it wasn't necessarily for the better. By early July of 1995, the number-one album on the *Billboard* charts was *Cracked Rear View*, by a new band from South Carolina, Hootie and the Blowfish. The group's feel-good, frat-boy rock and roll was about as meaningful and relevant to twenty-somethings as last week's keg party. Sure it was fun, but all it did was kill a few brain cells. It was hard to grasp the cosmic significance of songs with lyrics about the waste of getting wasted and swilling beer while feeling sorry for yourself.

Hootie and the Blowfish were the newest, hottest thing

in the record business but the band was nothing if not safe and predictable, and seemed to cater to aging baby-boomers who didn't mind hearing a new band so long as the music it cranked out wasn't particularly new.

It wasn't just Hootie that was making popular music seem so uninspired, though. In the same early July 1995 week that the band was number one in the charts, the soundtrack from the Disney film *Pocohantas* was number two and the new release for Jurassic rockers Pink Floyd, *Pulse*, had leapt in at number three.

There was really nobody reaching out to offer the Gen Xers something by, for, and about them. Nobody seemed willing to write music that would appeal to all demographics, and lyrics that would show everyone that there was more to this slacker generation than met the eye. When interviewed by the magazine *Who Cares* and the Washington-based think tank the Center for Policy Alternatives, 72 percent of the eighteen- to twenty four-year-olds surveyed believed that their generation "has an important voice, but no one seems to hear it." That might have been simply because there was nobody on a national scale speaking loudly enough to be heard.

And then, along came *Jagged Little Pill* and Alanis Morissette, who had entered the charts that same week Hootie sat at number one. Hers was a voice that was so strong and so sure, it couldn't be ignored. She was confident. She was authoritative. She cut straight to the point. And she was barely into her twenties. Alanis was the very sort of personality her generation could rally around—confident, defiant, and rather earnest—as a way of proving they weren't the lazy losers the press had made them out to be.

In "Hand in My Pocket," she admitted to being both lost and hopeful, realizing that eventually, life will turn out to be nothing but "fine, fine, fine." In "Not the Doctor," she proudly professed her independence from clingy lovers. In "Ironic," she recognized the contradictions of being alive but refused to get sucked down into an inescapable depression by it all. Alanis was taking charge of life in her songs, just as her generation was trying to do, even if they weren't given much credit by the outside world.

"*Jagged Little Pill* sold fifteen million copies because young people in this country were sufficiently angry with the way they were being perceived to turn to someone who understood that," explains *Billboard*'s White.

Plenty of critics portrayed her as the irritated symbol of a pissed-off generation, but to those who loved her music, it was a completely different story. Says one teenage fan, Jenn: "A great deal of people categorize Alanis as being angry or perverted, but I just can't see their reasoning. To me, her music is an expression of honesty . . . she is who she is and if you don't like it, tough. I think that is an image that women need these days."

Her strength was her realism. She knew that the troubles of youth everywhere couldn't be sugarcoated, but at the same time, they couldn't be considered insurmountable either. Though it certainly wasn't by design, Alanis had essentially become the latest winner in the "New Bob Dylan Sweepstakes." Every few years, it seems, writers and the public feel the need to unofficially tab somebody as the next singer/songwriter to define the lives and times of their peers in the personal way that Dylan had done for those who came of age in the 1960s. Some really did have an effect on the world, like Bruce Springsteen, while others now barely rank as a Trivial Pursuit question. (How many people can actually remember the likes of Steve Forbert?) It's often a heavy burden to bear, but it was now hanging around Alanis's neck.

That was the price she had to pay, though, because of the intensely personal nature of her lyrics, and the way the fans were embracing the honesty and poetry of those words. Like it or not, she was looked up to by the listeners and the media as spokesperson for her entire generation. It was not a job she particularly welcomed, but at the same time, she was as frustrated as any other Gen Xer about the way those under the age of thirty were being portrayed. So somebody had to speak up, and it might as well be someone who had seen it all even at a young age. Someone like herself.

"I see the whole concept of Generation X implies that everyone has lost hope," she once explained. "I can agree with that, and I can understand why, because of the fact that when my parents were coming out of high school or university with five or six jobs waiting for them, and people my age are coming out of university with a degree but . . . end up having no potential jobs and being in the same position as someone who left high school in grade 8. Just our times are different. So obviously, our mindsets are going to be different. But at the same time, I don't think that an entire generation should be underestimated."

She had faith in her peers, and they responded by placing all their faith in her. A lot of artists have fans. Alanis had fanatics. She wasn't just singing songs. She was telling truths that burrowed deep into their lives. Because she was dealing with issues and emotions that fellow Gen Xers could relate to, listening to *Jagged Little Pill* was sort of like getting a phone call from an old pal. They identified with her experiences, because she was the only one who really seemed to understand what they were going through.

"It feels like, spiritually, she is my best friend," believes one devout fan, Liza, who won't leave a store or a room if an Alanis song is playing in the background. "She has the same emotions as the rest of us. She goes through similar situations as the rest of us. She's no different."

Alanis wasn't just somebody for fans to listen to. She came across as somebody who would listen to them.

"Sometimes onstage I'm like a mirror," she once admitted. "My music becomes less about me and more about what the audience sees in me that reminds them of themselves. I sense that some are there to release tension and frustration, and that's gratifying."

Tim is perhaps the best example of how Alanis fans enjoyed taking that long, hard look in the mirror. The then-nineteen-year-old biological science student from Perth, Australia, had just graduated from high school in 1995, and was walking down a Sydney street when he passed a music store. In the window, a television set was showing the video for "Hand in My Pocket," which features an opening scene of Alanis standing out in the rain surrounded by people. Then he heard her words about feeling free yet focused, and couldn't help but feel that some way, somehow, she was also describing his feelings. He went inside, bought *Jagged Little Pill*, and hurried home to play it. His reaction was immediate and significant.

"I felt that her songs were very emotional, powerful, relaxing and releasing, and she expressed many things so clearly, things which I could not express with words before," he explains. That's why for days after he bought the CD, it was the first thing he listened to when he got up in the morning and the last thing he heard before going to bed every night. Personal problems had left him so depressed, he had begun to contemplate suicide. And then, he really started listening to "You Oughta Know."

At first, he figured it to be the angry, vengeful rock-and-roll rant that many critics had called it, but by really listening to it over and over, he decided the person who wrote it wasn't unlike him. In a sad and vulnerable mental state, with nobody to really listen and understand what the problem was.

"And by looking back now, I can say that this song saved my life, literally," says Tim. "I thought, 'If she was able to overcome her feelings and carry on with life, so can I.' I felt very connected with her, in a spiritual way."

He carefully studied every word she wrote, fascinated with the way she had been able to express herself so freely and take charge of her own life. With Alanis as his inspiration, he began to feel more positive and honest, and began to write poetry and mess around a little with songwriting. Not to become a professional performer necessarily, but just to try working out life's little problems in a more relaxed, more meaningful way.

More than a few rock stars achieve fame because, to a large degree, they *act* like stars. They wear outrageous outfits. They do provocative interviews and pose for outrageous photos. They date models. Their appeal is based on the fact that they live lives so different from the rest of us, you can't help but be in awe. Oh, and sometimes, you might even like to listen to their music. From Mick to Madonna, popular music has long been full of this sort of celebrity. They come in through the front door.

Alanis seemed to slip into popular culture from the service entrance. "She is more like a normal person I could talk to like a friend," says Dawn, an Ontario teen who has grown up listening to, and adoring, Alanis. "She is one out of millions of artists I see as *not* stuck up or a wee bit cocky or anything. She just looks, sings, dresses, and talks like a normal person, which is what drew me in. She doesn't try to look good and get made up, like most of them."

Adds sixteen-year-old Kathy, another devoted Alanis admirer: "She sings about the truth. She's not out to get money or adoration. She is very straightforward, she faces her fears, she is funny, she is honest, and she is beautiful (inside and out). Alanis and her songs have brought out all the things that have happened to me. I can relate to what she sings about. Everytime I hear her sing 'Perfect,' it makes me cry. I have gone through the same things, and still am. When I listen, and sing along, it's like I'm able to release all this pent-up anxiety."

It seemed that every fan was able to take one of Alanis's songs and find a way to make it about him- or herself. *Jagged Little Pill* was like rock-and-roll socialism, a CD for all the people. "You listen to the record and begin to feel like you had a hand in making it yourself because it seemed to relate to everyone's life," says White.

"The song that fascinates me the most is 'Perfect,'" explains another fan, Robert, who was seventeen when the CD first came out. "When I first heard it, I felt like she was saying all of the things that I was so afraid to say to my parents. . . . 'You Learn' had a major impact on my life. That song set off bells in my mind. I just felt it was time to break loose and live my own life. I moved eight hundred miles away from home."

The same song had a similar impact on Jenn, who first heard it on her fourteenth birthday. "I've been in some negative situations in my life, where at the time everything in life looked like it couldn't get any worse, but only in retrospect did I realize how grateful I was that I went through those experiences," she explains.

Alanis's fans were taking her music very personally, but at the same time, they all seemed quite eager to share their thoughts about her with each other. And they found the perfect way to do it. The Internet was the latest, and seemingly most essential, means of communication for many people in their teens and twenties. Since this was Alanis's target audience, it's not surprising that her position in pop culture was solidified on the World Wide Web. She was everywhere on it. Even more than two years after the release of *Jagged Little Pill*, you could type Alanis's name into a search engine like Yahoo! and come up with more than ninety different Internet fan sites devoted to her. Most treated her with total reverence, featuring all sorts of photos, news articles, and, most importantly, chat rooms where every detail of her life and career were discussed, no matter how trivial it might seem to outsiders.

Everyone had his or her own, often very different, reasons for starting up an Alanis Web site or at least coming to visit one of the many newsgroup bulletin boards. First and foremost, they were a sort of modern-day trading post, a place to exchange ideas and merchandise promoting their favorite singer. Sometimes the messages could be quite poignant, such as one from an Alanis fan whose dog was going to be put to sleep if she didn't raise money for its life-saving surgery. She called upon her fellow fans to buy some of her Alanis paraphernalia, like bootleg concert tapes and videos, in order to acquire the needed funds.

More often, though, the messages were a lot more frivolous. It was just fans sounding off on whatever subject popped into their heads. "The thing that I like most about Alanis Morissette is her leather and PVC trousers. I'm afraid that's all. But she does look extraordinarily sexy in them," read a posting on one Alanis electronic bulletin board.

"I'd hate to start another bickering match, but I read somewhere that Alanis admits to being bisexual. There's nothing wrong with that. I'm bi and just as human as everyone else," explained another, prompting a reply protesting that "who really cares if Alanis is bisexual or not? I mean, does it really matter? Does it affect your life that much?"

If you're going to be a cultural icon, though, you're going to have to take the bad with the good. Alanis was no exception, with several Web sites such as the People against Alanis Morissette's Music page popping up from time to time. "There's too much undue hype and 'oooh-ahhhing' over Alanis Morissette," the site's mission statement explained. "And for what? Nothing! Her music is crap. It is not in the least creative, nor entertaining. Her lyrics are as insightful as the O.J. trial." Visitors to the home page were encouraged to "call your local radio station when it plays Alanis tunes, and tell them how much she sucks."

Another site, which billed itself as offering "the Truth about Alanis," was a tirade against the singer that attacked her for everything from turning down interview requests with the press in her home country, to her misuse of the word "ironic," to her apparently unwashed hair. The criticism was scathing, but in a way, this only made Alanis seem even more culturally significant. They wouldn't bother going after you if they didn't consider you big and important enough to deal with. She had, in fact, become so influential that her icon status was having an effect on the music business itself.

"She started a trend," says another Canadian female singer/songwriter, Calgary native Jann Arden. "When 'You Oughta Know' went through the roof, the labels started scrambling and signing people within a month."

"Alanis proved to the business people that women rockers could be huge," explains White. "Women were writing better songs and leading better bands. It became an accepted thing."

This wasn't some sort of feminist movement in music, with women venting their anger about a male-dominated world. Such a critique was too one-dimensional, and usually came from men. This estrogen-fueled revolution was more complex than that, by praising "the ordinariness of women," as White puts it. It didn't hurt, adds Michael Greene from the National Academy of Recording Arts and Sciences, that as a result of the early groundwork laid by veterans such as Sinead O'Connor and Melissa Etheridge, "there was a stronger crew of women out there. And they were all saying important things."

By the time *Jagged Little Pill* was two years old, there would be all sorts of new names peppering the Top 200 album charts. Some of those who suddenly started to make some waves had been around long before Alanis had made it big, like Tori Amos and Sarah McLachlan. Others, like Joan Osborne, were struggling along on a parallel path, waiting to be discovered. Then there were performers like Meredith Brooks, Jewel, Fiona Apple, and even the Spice Girls, who seemed to benefit from the light Alanis's success was shining on other women in music. Their styles were often completely different. Amos's spare sound and often nonsensical lyrics were nothing like MacLachlan's dreamy folk style, which would never be confused with Apple's torch song–tinged rock or the Spice Girls' vanilla-flavored hip-hop.

Would any or all of these people have made it on their own if there had been no Alanis Morissette sitting atop the charts and demonstrating that a tough woman could sell as many records as any guy? Or had they, like her, just come along at a time when females in rock could all command more respect in our society? Nobody will ever know. Still, this new breed of popular female artist did have three things in common with Alanis, all of which now made them much more marketable. They were women. They were writing songs that boiled over with messages of personal empowerment. And this material was always catchy enough to win over a mass audience.

Much of the music that came from this female revolution was quite good, or at least very interesting. However, singer Arden was quick to observe that this rush to ink new female musicians might actually begin to sap the strength of the women-in-rock movement. What was once being done for the sake of art could now be created for the sake of commerce. Labels wanted somebody who could sound and sell like Alanis, so that's what many young writers would try to give them, instead of focusing on what they themselves really wanted to do.

"I see it all the time. I hear a lot of demo tapes and if I hear one more person throwing in that little hip-hop beat . . ." says an exasperated Arden, who had some limited post-Alanis success herself in 1996 with the adult-contemporary hit single "Insensitive." "Every new female artist has that sound, it seems."

While Alanis may have proved that female rockers were commercially viable, that isn't always such a good thing. For every Fiona Apple, who started out following Alanis's footsteps but quickly wandered off in a direction of her own choosing, there was a Meredith Brooks, whose Alanis-like looks and lyrics yielded only one hit single with the song "Bitch" before she faded from the top of the charts. Some made it. Some were just being ground up and spit out.

"I don't think women are better off," says Arden. "She hasn't had a hugely positive impact. You saw the industry signing these young girls like crazy after Alanis hit, but they couldn't give a shit about building up someone's career."

They wanted anger. They wanted venom. And they wanted it to sell by the bucketload. Arden says she and some of her peers began to feel rather typecast. It was rather an ironic (for lack of a better word) twist for Alanis. She'd spent all that time meeting with record companies, trying to get them to take a chance on a young female singer who wrote highly personal material. Now, those songs had proven to be more universal than personal, and all those labels that had spurned her were now after anyone who sounded like her. The alternative had become the mainstream.

This wasn't necessarily good news for Alanis. She was now so overexposed, her every move was open to criticism. That popularity was also reason for some of her peers to not take her work seriously. Even a veteran like Joni Mitchell, a fellow Canadian whose music Alanis had always loved, reportedly felt that "I'm a musical explorer and not just a pop songwriter or an occasional writer of a song or half a song, like these other women. Alanis Morissette writes words, someone else helps set it to music and then she's kind of stylized into the part."

Nor was this good news for other up-and-coming female musicians. No matter how good, or bad, their material was, it had to be judged against what Alanis had already done. Arden soon found that whenever she did an interview, the subject of Alanis Morissette always came up at one point or another, leaving her wondering whether any of what she was trying to say in her music was being heard.

When the Alanis Press Web site interviewed Meredith Brooks about the inevitable comparison between her and Alanis, she bluntly told the reporter: "Well, I was thinking, 'Could we get through this whole interview and not be asked about Alanis Morissette? I look forward to the day when that just doesn't happen anymore." Hers was a text-book example of what would happen to new women in rock during the months and years following the release of *Jagged Little Pill.*

If there ever was a case of someone whose success seemed a direct result of Alanis's, Brooks seemed to be it. With their thin frames and long dark hair, they looked somewhat alike. And with her risqué ranting (even flaunting of a naughty word right there in the title) in her hit single, "Bitch," it certainly did seem like musical history was re-peating itself. Brooks acknowledged to her interviewer that when she first heard Alanis sing, she even thought, "Oh good! Someone who sings like me!"

As far as she was concerned, any similarities between herself and Alanis were purely coincidental. "I think that when there is a good idea, there's just a good idea in the universe. . . . The idea came exactly at the same time to two people across the world," was her theory. In other words, you can't just tell someone to crank out intimate material like this. It has to come from one's own life experiences. That didn't stop certain executives at the label Arden re-corded for, A&M Records, from urging her to "come out swinging on my next record," just like Alanis had, she says. "But that anger thing doesn't represent me. To be fair, at least Alanis never said she was representing anyone but herself."

Nonetheless, Alanis has altered the expectations for other women. Arden couldn't help shake the feeling that there was a fair amount of "pressure definitely there, knocking on the door," for other women to do at least a portion of what Alanis had done both creatively and financially.

Although these other performers might have been getting a bit toasted in the wake of her heat, Alanis was too busy to really take notice. At the end of 1995, only a bit more than a year since she'd been so unsure of herself as an artist that she'd had a breakdown on the airplane home to Canada, Alanis was still trying to remain focused on her music and her devoted fans instead of on her newfound influence on the popular music landscape. That's what had gotten her here, and it was the only thing that really counted to her in the end. After all, hadn't she achieved quick, massive success once before, only to see it all abruptly fade from view as quickly as Right Said Fred's career?

The next year of her life, however, would make it impossible for her to remain oblivious to her own success any longer.

Ten

*I*t was the start of a brand new year, a time usually spent taking stock of one's life and figuring out how to become a more accomplished person by the time another 365 days slip by. Unless you're Alanis Morissette, in which case you would be running out of ways to prove yourself by about Presidents Day.

The year began with news that *Jagged Little Pill* was closing in on five million in sales in the United States and eight and a half million worldwide. Not only that, Alanis had been named both Best Female Singer and Best New Female Singer by the readers of *Rolling Stone*. The magazine's Critics' Poll had her trailing only P. J. Harvey in the Artist of the Year category, and "You Oughta Know" was tabbed as the third best single of 1995, trailing Coolio's "Gangsta's Paradise" and Edwyn Collins's "A Girl Like You." Meanwhile, in the readers' side of the poll, Alanis's single had the distinction of being voted Best Single while also showing up in the Worst Single category as well.

Over in England, she was nominated and would soon win the Best International Newcomer Award. Back home in Canada, she was up for five more prizes at the Juno Awards, including Female Vocalist of the Year, Best Rock

Album, Album of the Year, Single of the Year, and Best Songwriting (with Ballard).

At the same time that she was collecting these accolades, the National Academy of Recording Arts and Sciences announced the finalists for its thirty-eighth annual Grammy Awards and Alanis's name was exceedingly prominent. She received six nominations for her work on *Jagged Little Pill*, tying Grammy veteran Mariah Carey for most nominations. Alanis was up for Album of the Year, Best New Artist, Song of the Year, Best Rock Album, Best Female Rock Vocalist, and Best Rock Song.

This was big news. Though Alanis was getting honored all over the world, these nominations were something different. The Grammys had long been accused of taking the easy way out, of honoring recording artists who stayed squarely in the middle of the road. Commercial success seemed to be more rewarded than artistic merit. This was a group that had routinely handed out statuettes to less-than-cutting-edge performers like Michael Bolton, Phil Collins, and Whitney Houston in recent years, so the fact that such a purposely mainstream organization had opened its eyes and recognized Alanis's abilities was a major coup.

How did she celebrate this big news? Champagne, maybe? A party? A self-pat on the back? Not quite. The day the Grammy nominations were announced, Alanis sat in the women's locker room at the University of California at Irvine, getting ready for yet another concert in a tour that had now been going since the previous April. To her, this was all just business as usual.

So what if Madonna and Maverick had sent her a $25,000 Cartier watch to celebrate her success? Isn't it nice that President Bill Clinton told an interviewer about his desire to catch Alanis's performance on the Grammys? Who cares if her "Ironic" was now a hit single, with an accompanying music video that seemed to air about every ten minutes on MTV? Nothing seemed to faze her. This was really just her disco days revisited, no more and no less nerve-wracking.

"I can see how people in this business get freaked out

by success, but one reason I think I have been able to avoid that is that I already went through it on a much smaller scale in Canada,'' she told an interviewer the evening of her Grammy nods.

There was electricity practically crackling in the air everywhere she went, with *Jagged Little Pill* leaping back to number three on the *Billboard* charts after the Grammy nominations poured in and concerts kept selling out. The reviews were getting ever more respectful. Whereas the *New York Times* review of her show several months earlier had been polite but rather noncommittal, the paper was now as gushy as this stolid publication ever got.

Times critic Neil Strauss raved that her music was real enough to make her ''as much a conscience for the introverted world of today's rock audience as folk music was a voice for the extroverted world of the generation before.'' He also praised her for her ''powerful voice, frank lyrics about love and sex and a determination to assert her individuality,'' and figured that she was ''a one-woman release valve for the emotions of the young, jilted, alienated and confused.''

All of whom experienced anything but those emotions at an Alanis show. Her concerts were more like love-ins. Male fans came to her shows to offer her personal artifacts, like the woodpecker feather and Indian cutting stone one man brought to a gig in Manhattan, and to propose marriage. Female fans just watched and worshipped. Joyous fans inflated condoms and smacked them in the air. This was a party as much as it was a performance.

Nonetheless, Alanis wanted to keep her life as unplugged as possible. At most rock concerts, backstage is normally a smoky, drug- and alcohol-fueled whirlwind of roadies, groupies, record company hangers-on, and the like. Not so at an Alanis performance, where backstage was more like a reception for an author at some New Age bookstore. The air in her dressing room would be thick with the scent of aromatherapy candles. Tables were filled with fruit and vegetables. Bottled water was the drink of choice. Sometimes there might be the latest book she was reading, such as a tome about Buddhism or Tom Robbins's funky 1976 novel, *Even Cowgirls Get the Blues*'' (''Every twenty pages or so, there's just the most profound paragraph that keeps you going,'' she has said of the latter).

Whenever she had a chance, Alanis would find a peaceful place to sit and meditate. During the day leading up to a concert, she'd drink four bottles of ginseng and do all sorts of exercises, including a healthy amount of yoga. This was all her way of trying to get centered. When she went out there onstage, she had to be focused on what she was doing. The message in her words was too important to just go out and sleepwalk through a show. So, to get herself and everyone in the band ready, she developed a pre-gig ritual. Before heading out to perform, everyone would gather in a circle and Alanis would talk, sometimes for a couple of minutes.

Often, she would try to find time to keep her set fresh by creating some new tunes. Since her lyrics had to be very personal and contemplative, working on songs with dozens of people traipsing in and out of the backstage area proved to be difficult at best.

''In order to go to that place spiritually—that stream-of-consciousness, unfettered, unjudged place where I write lyrics from—I need to be somewhere less public,'' she told an interviewer while on tour.

The problem, however, was that she had a need to keep creating and little time to do so on the road. She decided to make the most of those hours spent backstage before a concert. Whenever she could arrange it, a side room would be set up at a venue so she could quietly collect her thoughts and develop new material. Just in case something good came out of the sessions, she arranged to have four amps, a pseudo–drum kit, and a portable eight-track recorder on hand.

This was an important period for her. Critics continued to suggest that Ballard was the real force behind the music on *Jagged Little Pill*, so by writing without him, Alanis could come up with songs that left no doubt about her own creative abilities. She still tended to fall back on collabo-

rators, though. Specifically, her own band, who had decided
to adopt the moniker Sexual Chocolate. Often at a sound-
check before a show, they would jam and she would sing
along and a new tune would grow out of this.

Sometimes this approach worked, with new numbers like
"No Pressure over Cappuccino," a ballad about Alanis's
twin brother, Wade, and "Can't Not," a powerful defense
of her right to complain, starting to pop up in performance.
And sometimes this approach didn't work, because the
writing process was kept too loose.

"What's really weird about her—and it's both good and
bad—is that she'll never come out and say, 'This is what
I'm going to do, and I'm going to use you and you and
you, and we're going to do this and this and this,' " Tobias
once explained. Instead, she never seemed concerned about
where the next good co-writer was coming from. She'd tell
her band she just wanted to start working on material and
whatever good songs emerged, no matter whether they were
hers, Glen Ballard's or the band's, she'd try to use them in
the show or on her next CD.

It shouldn't have been much of a surprise that she ran
such a loose ship when it came to writing on the road. After
all, *Jagged Little Pill* had been put together in much the
same way, just sitting around and brainstorming until an
idea spontaneously swooped in and possessed her psyche.
That didn't necessarily mean that her new tunes would pack
the same punch. Back when she was writing with Ballard,
she used songs like "You Oughta Know" to work through
a tortured love life. The anger fueled her creativity. But
now, while out on the road, she had discovered romance.

Actually, it was odd that it had taken this long for any
news to surface about who she was dating. Stars of her
magnitude usually became fixtures on the covers of super-
market tabloids, with every fling well documented by
grainy photographs of their first kiss from a new lover. This
had certainly happened to her boss, Madonna, the last female singer to have the kind of cultural impact Alanis was
having.

"We're both aggressive women and some men have difficulty responding to us because we don't want to be dominated or seduced in the typical ways," she said after spending "a couple of girlie nights" out with Madonna, talking about boys. "Every time a woman wants to assert herself and have an equal relationship, she's automatically considered to be a bitch."

All of the sexuality she'd kept hidden while growing up Catholic, and had only started to explore as she began her *Jagged Little Pill* tour, was now in full flower. Her life, she admitted, had become rather "deviant and perverse." Still, it wasn't until she'd been on the road several months that rumors of a serious romance surfaced in the gossip columns. Her personal life was now public knowledge, the best indication that she was now a full-fledged superstar.

The *New York Post* broke the news that Alanis had taken up with one Christian Lane. He was the lead singer/guitarist for Chicago-based Loud Lucy, a new and highly touted band that included Tommy Furar on bass and Marc Doyle on drums. Their debut disc had been released by Geffen Records, and it was good enough to land them a coveted opening slot for Alanis and her band. They were on the road together in the late summer of 1995, and then hooked up again at the end of the year.

This wasn't the first rock-and-roll romance for Lane. He had reportedly been dating Louise Post, who was one of the leaders of the alterna-chick Chicago band Veruca Salt, which had recently racked up a lot of attention and airplay thanks to the hit tune "Seether." Within a few weeks of being out on tour with Alanis, the rumors began to circulate that that affair was history and he had moved from Post to make time with the hottest female singer in the business.

The chemistry between the two performers was obvious to anyone who observed them together backstage. It wasn't anything overt, just a sense that something was going on by watching how they acted around each other. Alanis was smitten, but cautious. In her music, she could be free and spontaneous, but when it came to relationships, that was another story altogether.

"I've been seeing someone I really like, but I still don't

know how ready I am for big commitments," she admitted
later in the tour, without ever acknowledging whether or
not it was Lane she was speaking of. "I just want to focus
on enjoying a caring relationship. I'm really good at being
close to women and I'm trying to get better at being close
to men."

She was apparently easing into this gender adjustment
rather slowly, telling another interviewer that she and her
newfound love were "both kind of androgynous: we're
both she-males in this relationship. It's very balanced."

It didn't take long for Lane to become quite tight with
Alanis's band as well, and soon he began riding in their
tour bus while the rest of Loud Lucy trailed behind in a
smaller, shabbier van. As his relationship with the singer
got more intense, it seemed to some that he had infiltrated
Alanis's camp so much that it was almost like he'd become
a member of her group.

Soon, those around Lane began to notice that something
was different. He had long been a talented alternative artist
happy working outside of the mainstream, but hanging
around with Alanis was changing his tune. Suddenly, his
status as a struggling singer/songwriter just wasn't good
enough for him. The lifestyle of a chart-topping performer
was too seductive to resist.

"I know he truly liked her, he was intoxicated by her
lifestyle," says one observer. "That caused a little bit of
tension in his band. He separated himself from them rather
quickly."

"He couldn't deal with the fact that he wasn't huge,"
adds another acquaintance of Lane's. "His record could
have been big, but it would have taken time to break. He
just saw how huge Alanis was and didn't understand how
much work she had put into it."

The love affair with Alanis would continue, on and off,
long after Lane's band stopped opening for her. His relationship with his band, however, would not. The animosity
generated by his association with Alanis put too much of
a strain on Loud Lucy, and the group broke up after selling
a skimpy fifty thousand copies of their debut. "They told

us the album would sell itself, and when everything didn't happen the way they said it would, a lot of tension developed," Lucy drummer Doyle would explain. "We decided to end it before everyone completely hated each other." Lane moved out to Southern California, where he could be near Alanis after her tour ended, and set to work on making a solo album.

Even as Alanis's success was having an adverse effect on her beau's band, her career continued to pick up steam as it rolled along and headed into Los Angeles for the 1996 Grammy Awards. She had been asked to perform "You Oughta Know" live at the ceremony, being held at the Shrine Auditorium, and workers began getting the stage ready to accommodate her and the rest of her band.

"We designed a stage pretty consistent with what she was," says Ken Ehrlich, director of the Grammy telecast, of the basic, brightly lit set originally constructed for Alanis's performance. "Then, when we saw her in rehearsal, I said, 'We want to change this.'"

That's because Alanis had come to the run-through with some ideas of her own. Along with her manager and the Grammy producers, she had decided to do something special and different with her performance. As she stepped onstage and began to sing, it was apparent something new was happening. She was accompanied not just by her band, but also by Ballard on piano and a string quartet. Everyone who had been milling around, getting ready for a show that was only two days away, stopped in their tracks and stared at the petite young woman with the long, dark hair. The auditorium grew very silent as Alanis began to sing her trademark tune with a slow, somber arrangement that gave it a completely new meaning.

Instead of sounding angry and vengeful, this acoustic version of "You Oughta Know" came across as melancholy and regretful. Her voice was softer, Lashley's guitar more subtle, the piano and strings very comforting. After months of performing the song as some sort of hard-rock anthem, doing it this way offered Alanis a chance to bring it back closer to the way it began.

"The song helped me honestly release how I felt without censoring myself to get it out of my system," she later said. "The acoustic version taps into the original emotion that inspired the song in the first place."

Whether it was simply the shock of hearing the tune done so differently, or the way its meaning had shifted so dramatically, it was clear something special was going on. Ehrlich agreed with Scott Welch that the standard set and lighting wouldn't have been right for this performance.

"As soon as she started singing, I looked at her and said, 'Candelabras,' because it seemed like a baroque interpretation of the song," Ehrlich recalls. "Her management asked us about putting down some rugs, so we did that too."

Once the right look was established for her performance, there was still one more problem that had to be addressed. CBS would be airing the Grammys live to half of the country (it would be on tape in the Mountain and Pacific time zones), and there was that nasty use of the F word to deal with. Many radio stations had simply bleeped out the offending verb when they played it, but the National Academy of Recording Arts and Sciences wanted to leave it in for the telecast.

"We had an interesting situation. Was CBS going to bleep her?," says NARAS president Greene. "I had a long talk with CBS Entertainment president Les Moonves about it and said, 'If this was a gratuitous use of the word, you could do what you want, but this is integral to the song.'"

CBS understood the argument. The network didn't ask her to change the way she was going to perform her hit. When she came to the offending bit of lyric, she didn't hold back. In the end, though, it didn't matter. She spoke the word. The producers bleeped it out. Only lip-readers were able to appreciate what she had done.

In the end, with or without the "fuck," her performance was a real stunner. With all the bluster that usually dominates awards shows, the sight of this purportedly pissed-off young singer surrounded by soft candlelight was quite a pleasant contrast. The kinder, gentler "You Oughta Know" was the highlight of the evening and became such a hot ticket, a recording of it would eventually be released by Maverick.

That wouldn't be the last time Alanis was onstage that night, either. She won in four of the six categories for which she was nominated, going home with awards for Album of the Year, Best Rock Album, Best Rock Song, and Best Female Rock Vocal Performance.

The Album of the Year honor was particularly impressive. In past years, many highly respected rock bands, like R.E.M. and U2, had been nominated for but failed to win that top prize, losing out to softer, safer pop performers like Natalie Cole and Whitney Houston. By taking Alanis seriously, Grammy voters were letting the public know it was time to start taking these awards more seriously.

This was an evening of vindication for the singer. Not only had *Jagged Little Pill* become an amazing commercial success, it had been given the stamp of approval by Alanis's fellow musicians. After all the struggles she'd been through to get to this place, after all the critical put-downs she'd endured, going all the way back to her first two CDs, Grammy night was the time to get even. She could stand up at the podium, accept her accolades, and mock those who had written her off.

But gloating was simply not her way. It never had been. Instead, she simply got up onstage and announced, "I accept this on behalf of anyone who's ever written a song from a very pure place." She showed more enthusiasm when her childhood idol, Annie Lennox, won the Best Female Pop Vocalist award, pumping her fist in the air.

Backstage after the show, she was even more reticent to speak. Sticking with her plan to do as few interviews as possible, Alanis made herself completely unavailable to the throng of reporters on hand to cover the event. Her management had made it clear to CBS early on that she was already overexposed, and there would be no interviews at all on Grammy night. She showed up in the photo room for a brief time, so pictures of her gripping her statuette could be shipped out for the morning newspapers. After that, though, Alanis had left the building.

Awards meant about as much to her as yesterday's breakfast. They were taken in and then forgotten. There was a time not that long ago when winning might have meant everything to her, but that was before writing *Jagged Little Pill* taught her what was really important.

"When I was younger, I always used to think that if you were to have a number one record and win a Grammy award, your life would be wonderful," she later mused. "But the opposite is true. It's more a test of you. If your foundation is shaky, then being thrown into that lifestyle will break you."

She didn't hate her experience at the Grammys. She was just happy to get away from the adulation of her peers and back to the appreciation of her fans. Alanis would throw her trophies into her suitcase as if they were books she'd get around to skimming some other time.

"In the end, it's the show that counts," Tobias has said. "That's possibly the biggest trophy of all, when the kids from high school actually tell her their heart is with her."

Alanis may not have given the Grammys a second thought. The record-buying public, however, felt differently. No doubt spurred on by the attention generated by her victories, *Jagged Little Pill* regained the top spot on the *Billboard* charts within a couple of weeks after the awards show. It would spend nearly all of the next two months there, getting bumped to number two only once, in favor of the *Beatles Anthology 2*.

Meanwhile, back in Ballard's home state of Mississippi, the House of Representatives passed a resolution honoring its native son for his good work on the album and "You Oughta Know." Unfortunately, these conservative politicians voted without ever having paid attention to the song's lyrics. Once they did that, Ballard's honor was stripped from him as quickly as it had been given.

But the great award parade wasn't over for him or Alanis. And as prestigious as the Grammys were, the Junos had even more significance. They represented a homecoming of sorts, an opportunity to return triumphant to the land where she'd had her first successes and greatest disappointments. Alanis's career path in the four years since she'd won the Most Promising Female Vocalist prize—bottoming out with the musical style that earned her the award and coming back with something that went 180 degrees in a different direction—probably wasn't quite what Juno voters had in mind.

Introduced by Anne Murray as "perhaps the most honest voice to ever come out of Ottawa" (something all the politicians in the Canadian capital probably didn't enjoy hearing), a leather-clad Alanis came onstage, accompanied by thunderous applause, to sing a chilling, energetic version of "Ironic" that was a sharp contrast to her subdued Grammy appearance. Not that she needed to prove herself to the home-country crowd of ten thousand, but her performance demonstrated precisely how much she had changed from that big-haired teenager who not so long ago gushed in her postcard home about all the awards hoopla.

By the end of the evening, any doubts Alanis might have had about being welcomed back were swept away as she copped five major awards, including Single of the Year for "You Oughta Know," Female Vocalist of the Year, Songwriter of the Year (along with Ballard), Album of the Year, and Rock Album of the Year. When she stepped up onstage to accept the latter honor, it was the perfect forum for revenge. She had heard all the criticism from people like the Toronto deejay who scoffed at the validity of her image change. Juno night, just like Grammy night a couple of weeks earlier, would have been the perfect time to strike back. Instead, as she always had, Alanis decided to cruise along the high road.

"Most people's growth is done in private," she told the crowd at Hamilton, Ontario's Copps Coliseum. "An artist's is done in public. I thank Canada for accepting that in me."

She continued the conciliatory tone a few minutes later, when she went back up to accept the Songwriter of the Year award. "It's a pleasure to do what I do and to communicate it to you, so I thank you."

There was no bitterness, no smug I-told-you-so's. Coming to the Junos was like going back to the first office you worked in after leaving school. You enjoy being back on familiar turf but at the same time, you realize very quickly why it was that you had to move on from the place. Had Alanis stayed in Canada, the chances were slim that *Jagged Little Pill* would ever have been created. That country's music business would no doubt have continued to typecast her, and she might have eventually succumbed to that.

This was abundantly clear to her by the time she went backstage for interviews, another divergence from her Grammy game plan. "I needed to travel," she explained. "I had to get out of my comfort zone."

Leaving Canada had allowed her to start her life and her music over again, something she had done exceedingly well. She had been so successful, though, another problem now presented itself. Alanis had essentially traded one comfort zone for another. *Jagged Little Pill* was now heading on toward the ten million sales mark. She had won just about every award she could possibly snag. Her tour was going strong, and wouldn't be over for nine more months. This was as comfy as it gets for a rock star.

If there was one thing Alanis had never wanted to be, though, it was a rock star. That was the whole point behind everything from keeping a low profile with the media to holding onto her tiny Santa Monica apartment. One of the many joys of *Jagged Little Pill* was the way her lyrics expressed the thoughts and feelings many people experience but seldom speak about, and if she began to believe her success, she might lose touch with the real life her fans were living.

Perhaps it was no coincidence, then, that her trip up to Canada for the Junos included a stop back home in Ottawa. Here was the chance to remember her roots. To some citizens, she was the returning hero. To others, she was a musical opportunist. To herself, she was just an Ottawa girl getting back to where she once belonged.

Eleven

Jacquelin Holzman had the best of intentions. She felt it was her duty, as both mayor of Ottawa and an acquaintance of Alan and Georgia Morissette, to find some way the city could celebrate the return of one of its most successful former citizens. It had been twenty-four years since Ottawa's last big singing sensation, Paul Anka, came back home to receive a ceremonial key to the city. Perhaps, Holzman theorized, it was time to give Alanis the same honor.

She would be arriving in town in early March for a performance at the four-thousand-seat Congress Centre, her first show in her hometown since the release of *Jagged Little Pill* nearly a year earlier, so a plan was put in place. In the afternoon before the concert, Alanis would be presented with a plaque that contained the key, and then conduct a press conference to announce a Canadian tour she had planned for later in the year.

Even though Alanis had already been given a truckload of trophies, Holzman figured this one would be special. "Deep down, people like to be recognized by their hometown," she said.

Unfortunately, though, the hometown wasn't entirely enthusiastic about recognizing Alanis. Many Ottawa radio stations were still reluctant to play any music from *Jagged Little Pill*, falling back on the explanation that her songs didn't fit their demographics. And when Holzman made her announcement, at least one local television station, CJOH, was flooded with calls from residents who wanted to vent their frustration about it.

It wasn't just her music that bothered them. Some people had been upset by interviews she had done in which she claimed, among other things, that the environment she worked in as a teenager reduced her songwriting to something menial, leaving her feeling too helpless to resist.

"I know for a fact that she's bruised a lot of egos in Ottawa . . . saying, 'Well, I was controlled by others,' " according to Don Marcotte, a producer at CJOH who had worked on a documentary about Alanis years earlier and befriended the young singer. "I know a lot of the people she's been alluding to [who] don't feel that way at all. They feel it was a creative endeavor, and they're saying, 'Well, Jesus, it sure wasn't presented like that to us at the time. We sure didn't feel like we were controlling her.' "

Her grade 9 English teacher, MacGregor, understood where the bitterness was coming from. Anybody could have forecast this would eventually happen, since it had been going on for years, going all the way back to when she was attending Glebe and dealing with the icy behavior of some of her classmates. It was jealousy, pure and simple. Plenty of people had a secret dream of becoming a world-renowned rock and roll singer, and "if you elevate that one thousand times, you get to where Alanis is now and they're envious. It's their fantasy and she's living it."

Still, even some who had no reason to be jealous seemed put off by Alanis now that she had made it big. Louise Reny, who along with Leslie Howe had been instrumental in helping Alanis put her very first album together, had continued to release records, first as part of Sal's Birdland and, later, Artificial Joy Club. Her career was going just fine, but she felt abandoned by the girl she once mentored.

"We used to be friends, but she hasn't called me since she's become a star," she would vent to a reporter. "I

helped out this little kid who used to idolize me, helped her
in the studio. I let her come up onstage with me and even
lent her my stage clothes. What more can I do for somebody? And when they come to town, they don't even call
you? Like, get your secretary to call me. Maybe remember
my existence.''

Not all of those who helped Alanis on her way up felt
the same way. David Baxter, who had written with her and
befriended her during her days in Toronto, continued to
chat with her whenever their schedules allowed. When they
were both in New York at the same time, he even bought
a bag of CDs he thought she might like and dropped them
off at her hotel, forgetting that he had absentmindedly taken
the piece of gum he had been chewing and stuck it into the
bag as well. It wasn't long before the phone in his own
hotel room rang, and he heard Alanis's voice.

''Thanks for the gum,'' she told him with a laugh.

She was still the same free-spirited, teasing young
woman whose company Baxter had always enjoyed. Unfortunately, not everyone felt that way. Mayor Holzman
couldn't ignore this undercurrent of bitterness that was
drifting all around Ottawa, but she also didn't want to take
it too seriously. Most of it, she assumed, stemmed from
people who remembered Alanis as a perky, nonthreatening
young girl and couldn't accept that she had grown up,
toughened up, and moved away.

Holzman, however, admired the way Alanis had transformed from a cute, well-behaved kid who could sing pretty
well into ''a talented woman who had fought her way up.''
If there was anybody who could handle all of the criticism,
it was Alanis. After all, she'd spent months enduring the
barbs of her detractors down in the States. Getting through
the flak at home should be a piece of cake.

''She always had an ability to hold an audience,'' the
mayor recalls. ''She had a mind of her own, and was never
a wimpy child.''

Undaunted by the fuss surrounding her decision to give
Alanis the key to the city, Holzman issued this proclama-
tion declaring Alanis Morissette Day in Ottawa:

"Whereas rock singer and recording artist Alanis Morissette was born at the Riverside Hospital in Ottawa on
June 1, 1974; and whereas Ms. Morissette has achieved
international fame, critical acclaim and superstar status
through the success of her album, *Jagged Little Pill*, which
has so far sold over six million copies and earned Alanis
six Juno nominations and six Grammy nominations . . . ;
and whereas as a native daughter of Ottawa, Alanis Morissette is one of our city's great ambassadors to the world,
helping to shine the world's spotlight on her hometown and
joining the ranks of Ottawa's many artists and performers
who have brought honour and distinction to our city
through their contribution to the popular culture of our times;
and whereas it is the desire of this [city] Council, on behalf
of the people of Ottawa, to congratulate Alanis and demonstrate our pride in her achievements; therefore it is resolved
that . . . on the occasion of her first local performance since
the success of *Jagged Little Pill*, Ms. Morissette be awarded
the Key to the City in celebration of her success."

The ceremony/press conference went on as planned, and
without incident. Looking fresh and pleasant in a glittery
brown sweater, Alanis announced the details of the Canadian leg of her tour that would begin in midsummer. Then,
for the first time since she had become a star, she spoke to
Canadian reporters and explained that, "I just want to make
peace with where I came from."

She fielded the usual questions about the inspiration for
songs like "You Oughta Know" and the reasons for her
tremendous success. When asked about why there were still
people in Ottawa, including some former Glebe classmates,
who seemed upset by her accomplishments, Alanis politely
shrugged the complaints off.

"I don't think it's just Canada," she said. "I think it is
humans. You know, I think there are some people who have
difficulty with other people's success. That's part of life. I
don't think it is just Glebe."

This didn't silence her critics. Barely a week after her
visit to Ottawa, a new minicontroversy over "You Oughta
Know" emerged. The song had been included on a seventy

seven-track compilation, *Oh, What a Feeling—a Vital Collection of Canadian Music*, but no sooner had copies of the CD been shipped to retailers when its producers started hearing from angry consumers. They received dozens of complaints about the inclusion of a song that made specific use of an obscenity.

Rather than stand firm, they opted to rerelease the collection with a version of "You Oughta Know" that left out the offending epithet. "We made this decision . . . for an ethical reason," explained executive producer Randy Lennox. "I have to be aware of the person . . . that bought this collection and is playing it for his or her family."

At this point, telling Alanis of new concern about her music was sort of like telling Bob Dylan to enunciate. Been there, heard that, and it didn't make any difference. She would keep right on doing what she was doing, and if people were somehow offended or annoyed, there was always Celine Dion to listen to.

Alanis was making some changes in her life. During a brief break from her tour, she had returned to her Santa Monica apartment, packed up her belongings, and moved all the boxes into storage. She wasn't able to spend time there anyway because she was on the road, so it made no sense to keep the place anymore. Meanwhile, as spring turned to summer, the tour itself was changing, finally making the step up to larger venues.

This leg of her road show began in Portland, Oregon, with twenty thousand people packing into the Rose Garden. Playing in big arenas meant attracting a wider audience than she ever could in small clubs, and that was readily apparent as the concert began. The age range of the crowd was even greater now. There were ten-year-old girls wearing lipstick, pigtails, and men's sport coats, often accompanied by parents or guardians. After all, some of Alanis's lyrics were rated R.

She still seemed a bit quiet up on the stage, and at least one local reviewer, Erik Flanigan, noticed that she seemed a bit awkward as she skipped around the large stage.

Though she lacked "a commanding physical presence," he observed, the enthusiastic audience didn't seem to mind a bit. Even when she stumbled a bit with her harmonica and guitar-playing, she drew cheers anyway.

Which, to Flanigan, was the key to her appeal. She had long explained that there was really no division between her and her fans. Whether it was on her CD or on a stage, she was simply a reflection of who they were and what they were thinking. Giving a rough, unpolished performance made her seem more human, more like everyone else. The size of the concert halls may have gotten grander, but Alanis was still trying to keep everything else as simple as possible when she went out there to sing.

The same held true backstage as well. When the alternative pop band Imperial Drag opened for her on the West Coast swing of the tour, the band's guitarist, Eric Dover, was surprised to discover that Alanis was a low-key woman who liked to warm up for her shows by playing a game or two of Ping-Pong.

"You'd find her polishing her skills," he recalls. "She seemed to have a pretty good handle on the game."

She was also someone who, while not impressed by her own celebrity, could still be left a little awestruck by meeting a performer she admired. When Olivia Newton-John wandered backstage after Alanis performed at the Greek Theater in Los Angeles, she was cornered by the young singer, who gushed that Newton-John had been the one to inspire her interest in music many years earlier.

This wasn't the only star encounter of the summer. She was invited to travel to London and sing at Prince Charles's Trust Charity concert, an annual event that attracts some of rock's most legendary performers. This year's show was no exception. Alanis shared the bill with, among others, The Who, Bob Dylan, Eric Clapton, and the Rolling Stones' Ron Wood. Her life was already a long line of big events, but getting up in front of these artists, and a Hyde Park crowd of 150,000 people, had to be the biggest.

The opportunity left her feeling a bit nervous, unable to fully comprehend the meaning of being up there with someone like Dylan, whom her father had come of age listening to. Being asked to participate in this event was the ultimate compliment, a passing of the torch from one generation of rocker to the next. Once upon a time, her fellow performers had dared to be different. The emotional power of their work set them apart from their peers, and the listening public responded in droves. They were the rebels, the risk-takers whose songs had the power to infiltrate people's lives. Theirs was music with meaning. Until they themselves became the status quo.

Eventually, they couldn't avoid growing older and drifting out of touch with the sounds and issues that record-buying kids deem relevant. It was time for some young, radical soul to create music that carried on their tradition. The organizers of the Hyde Park benefit knew this, and they recruited Alanis as the new performer most likely to connect with a youthful audience no longer able to relate to someone like Dylan or Clapton. And, just maybe, the crowd might then be inspired to check out the classic work of these artists.

At the same time, Alanis's presence on this prestigious bill legitimized her work with the fans of these veterans. They may have once written her off as some one-hit Generation X wonder, but if she was now keeping this kind of company, perhaps she deserved another listen.

Just because she had achieved this career pinnacle, it didn't mean the rest of her tour would cruise along Easy Street, however. The critics of her work didn't go away. It had been that way from the very beginning of her career, so there was no reason to think it would stop just because she had been welcomed into the big leagues. The complaints were essentially the same as they'd always been, that Alanis was talented but a well-packaged version of alternative-rock rage that had been done better by commercially less successful performers.

Reviewing an Alanis concert for the *Chicago Tribune*, Alison Stewart griped that the singer's image "seemed cobbled together from those that have come before her: the frenetic stage-pacing comes courtesy of Eddie Vedder. . . .

vocal phrasings and angry-but-empathetic persona vary
little from those of underground folk star Ani DiFranco
that they have to be intentional, and her dead-on take on
sexual politics would never have been possible had Liz
Phair not gotten there first.''

Not all the criticism of her work was so harsh. In particular, two light-hearted music videos that gently ribbed her
own ''Ironic'' video started popping up on MTV. Alanis's
''Ironic'' had become a staple piece of programming for
the video channel, and used trick photography to feature
four different personalities of the singer going for a car ride.
The pleasant, concerned mother character sat in the driver's
seat, keeping an eye on the flirtatious girl, the wild child,
and the introspective daughter. Just as the clip was starting
to wear out its welcome, MTV began airing the two paro-
dies, which offered slightly different twists on the theme.

In the first, it wasn't just someone pretending to be a kid
sitting in the backseat of the car. It was a real five-year-old
girl, the daughter of the video's director as well as the niece
of an assistant production manager on Alanis's tour, reen-
acting all of the parts. Why? Because the director wanted
to give his sister a laugh.

In the second, the same basic scenario featured comedian
and Ottawa native Donal Logue playing a greasy-haired,
bespectacled cabbie who acted out the four characters. Instead of lip-synching the words to ''Ironic,'' he made up
some new lyrics, including, ''It's like meeting the girl of
your dreams . . . and finding out she's only five.''

''I'm a big fan,'' he would say of Alanis, ''but earnest
rock that purports to be intellectual deserves to get its ass
whupped.''

Still, imitation is the sincerest form of flattery, and Logue
wouldn't have bothered mocking Alanis if ''Ironic'' wasn't
so popular. Not to mention well respected, since it helped
her take home MTV awards for Best New Artist and Best
Female Video in early September.

Just as she had done at the Grammys several months
earlier, Alanis accepted her honors somewhat reluctantly.
''It still doesn't change the concept of art being judged,''

she groused at the ceremony. "I still don't agree with it."

Maybe this lukewarm response was just the result of award overload. Or perhaps it was just the fact that she'd spent most of the past year and a half out on the road. Whatever the reason, it seemed to at least some who spent time with her that Alanis was getting a bit worn down.

When she showed up for the MuchMusic Awards in Toronto a month later, where she'd been nominated for even more of those honors she didn't enjoy receiving, at least one music business insider noticed that there was something different about her. Something that hadn't been there before the *Jagged* little juggernaut began.

"She looked really unhappy, despondent, tired," he explains. "She had a circle of three or four females around her, and they were very protective of her. It was a sharp contrast to what I'd observed of her years before. I started to wonder if this was some sort of an act."

Her old friend from her MCA days, Cameron Carpenter, even noticed that she had changed somewhat. He still enjoyed her company, but he could sense that she "seemed a little weary of the fact that she couldn't just walk down the street anymore."

For better and worse, that was the price to be paid for the kind of success she continued to experience. *Jagged Little Pill* had reached another milestone, topping the twelve million sales mark and moving past Carole King's *Tapestry* (ten million), Madonna's *Like a Virgin* and Mariah Carey's *Music Box* (both at nine million) to tie Whitney Houston's 1985 self-titled disc as the top-selling album ever by a female artist. Now she was at number six on the all-time sales chart, far behind the top spot (Michael Jackson's *Thriller*, at twenty four million sold) but closing in on the likes of Bruce Springsteen, Elton John, and Garth Brooks.

That was the upside of Alanis-mania, which showed no signs of abating even as she finished the final U.S. leg of her tour and headed overseas one more time. The downside, however, was the increasing demands on her and her time. It had become increasingly difficult to find time for herself, away from record executives and managers and promoters and fans and even her band. That's the odd thing about being on tour for such a long period of time: You can be surrounded by dozens of people, but that doesn't stop you from feeling alone. This certainly accounted for at least some of the guarded behavior she had exhibited at the MuchMusic Awards.

"While it may have seemed like I was surrounded by allies, life on the road can be very insulated, therefore isolating," she said months after the tour ended. "There is no handbook on how to deal with road life and external success, much less how to dispel the illusion without seeming spoiled and ungrateful."

Meditation helped restore some of her sanity, offering her a few quiet moments to reflect on everything that had happened to her during the past year. Such introspection always yielded the same result. As she later explained, "Meditation, along with 'achieving' what could have seemingly been the 'ultimate achievements,' made me realize that we are all sadly and ignorantly chasing our tails."

She would be the first to admit that all this attention brought some good things. The opportunity to reach out to those who could benefit from some of the personal empowerment she preached in her music was certainly a big plus. And, let's face it, making a bit of money wasn't necessarily a bad thing.

"It's definitely good to have . . . if you have the right view of it," she admitted to an interviewer when the tour rolled into its next-to-last stop, New Zealand. "Money can give you freedom, money can give you peace of mind and security knowing that if and when I were to have children, in ten or however many years, that I can do that. . . . I don't know if I'll ever get married. I might, but I am definitely going to have children. Definitely!"

The times, they had a-changed. The woman who had first leapt to superstardom with a song about sexual betrayal was now seriously, and publicly, entertaining the thought of being a mother. Over the course of the previous eighteen months, she had gone from fiery young talent sowing her wild oats to self-confident young woman. Somewhere along the way, her life had turned around 180 degrees—again.

Way back when she was just starting out on the road, and *Jagged Little Pill* had yet to sell a single copy, she was just a young woman struggling to make sense of her life. She had grown up perhaps a bit too quickly, constantly appearing more like adult than child, skipping right past the time of fun and experimentation that is adolescence. What choice was there? Few people would take the music of a kid seriously, so she couldn't act like one. This was the only way to be if she wanted to succeed. And then, her career took that first nosedive.

Then, it became apparent that it was time to grow down instead of up. Maybe it was time to stop being the straight arrow everyone expected her to be, and start living for the moment. That was the spirit that carried her through those early days on the road, when she got to kick back and live the carefree life of a free-spirited rocker. Gradually, almost imperceptibly, though, things began to shift. And as Alanis and her band arrived in Honolulu and stormed the stage for their last performance, she had entered yet another new stage of her life. She had become, as she put it, a "leader, friend, mother, boss, child."

This wasn't just the finale of a tour for her. She had also come to the end of the journey of self-discovery that *Jagged Little Pill* was all about. Alanis wasn't just the album's singer and songwriter. She was also the chief recipient of its wisdom. There was really only one question that remained unanswered in her life.

Now what?

Twelve

*L*ea Thompson sat on the Pasadena, California, stage in
the summer of 1997, searching for the right way to explain
the phenomenon she was now a part of. Along with fellow
actresses Brooke Shields, star of the sit-com *Suddenly Susan*, and Sharon Lawrence, star of the sit-com *Fired Up*,
the star of *Caroline in the City* had come to talk with more
than one hundred TV reporters about NBC's bold new programming strategy of filling its Monday night schedule
with four female-oriented comedies. (*Naked Truth* star Téa
Leoni was apparently unavailable.)

This was something new, something no other network
had ever before experimented with in its fall lineup. And
she needed the perfect analogy to explain how times had
changed, and whereas this idea might once have seemed
radical and a sure way to lose viewers, it was now a perfectly valid notion. What better example was there than the
revolution that had only recently occurred in the world of
popular music?

"I was listening to the radio today and . . . I heard four
women singing—different artists—singing songs, back to
back," the actress eagerly told the writers. "And three
years ago, the wisdom was you couldn't put two women

singing back to back on the radio. You had a woman, then a man, and a man, and then a woman. But there were four women in a row and I went, 'That's so cool.' That's going to be like Monday night.''

Certainly Alanis couldn't take all the credit for the change Thompson was so excited about, but she was definitely a prime force in a diverse new wave of commercially successful women in popular music. Finally, in 1996, it wasn't just a man's world at the top of the charts. The ten best-selling albums for the year, according to the Recording Industry Association of America, included seven females or female-fronted acts with very different styles including Celine Dion, Mariah Carey, and No Doubt, with Alanis at the top of the list in terms of both sales (7.38 million for the year) and media attention.

Pill was now the best-selling nonsoundtrack disc ever from a female artist, with total sales reaching a staggering fifteen million. That meant she would pass the first records by Boston and Hootie and the Blowfish, and have the best-selling American debut disc in history (those Canadian CDs somehow never figured into this honor).

Alanis had gone from being an artist who had saved her career to a superstar who was singularly responsible for keeping the record industry afloat. The music business was in a severe stagnation through all of 1996, with sales barely up from the previous year. Major artists, from George Michael to Pearl Jam to R.E.M., had released albums that started off well but quickly slid down the sales charts. It was Alanis who was still drawing buyers into record stores, where they would inevitably browse and, shop owners hoped, purchase something in addition to *Pill*.

"Big hits are good for business. The music industry needs big, big hits," according to Danny Goldberg, who had seen plenty of performers come and go during his years running labels like Atlantic Records and Mercury Records and his own talent agency, Gold Mountain. "Alanis is a monster artist that keeps alive that dream of opportunity for other musicians. She shows everyone what is possible."

She still had her critics, of course, but now the attacks

had little to do with how genuine her music might be. By early 1997, she had become unpopular in some circles simply because she was so popular. In Chicago, for instance, local radio deejay Lou Brutus organized PUSMAC, aka People United to Stop Morissette the Anti-Christ. Anyone wishing to join got a membership card to prove their contempt for Alanis, along with a special certificate of merit explaining that members "will refrain from being Ironic, going down on people in theaters and thinking of Alanis Morissette while fucking anyone."

"She had reached the point where there was so much press about her, any message she had, had become meaningless," Brutus says. "Whatever she'd set out to do was lost in a sea of hype and she'd become this media thing, and I wanted to say something about that."

His ranting against Alanis was at least partially tongue-in-cheek. And a bit too late in the game. By the spring of 1997, Alanis was on an extended vacation from the music business. It was a strange feeling for her. After the grind of touring for a year and a half, after being a critical punching bag, after taking on the burden of being her generation's valedictorian, life was suddenly quiet. For the first time in her life, she had the chance to relax. There were no worries about moving up the next step in her career. She could finally stop and enjoy the fruits of her labor.

For instance, after years spent living in cramped apartments or out of boxes, she bought her first house, tucked away near the fashionable Brentwood area of Los Angeles. She picked the place, with its security gates, swimming pool, and backyard view of the Getty Museum, without ever going to look at it. Instead, she simply glanced at a video of homes up for sale.

"They showed me everything from places that were really small to places that were massive. . . . This was one of the smallest," she would explain.

Instead of going on a grand tour of the town to search for a mansion, she made this big investment with the casualness of someone ordering a pizza. Her bank account was large, but it made little impression on her. She was certainly generous when it came to others, buying a new home in Ottawa for her parents, for instance.

As for indulging herself, there were occasional shopping trips to the fashionable Santa Monica Promenade not far from her house. She'd stroll along, looking very casual and unassuming in overalls, sandals, and sloppy T-shirts as she picked out new clothes. Then, there were all the oak antiques and carved wooden floors she bought for her house.

Still, she hadn't written *Jagged Little Pill* in order to be a millionaire, so she saw little point in trying to live like one. When she went out to dinner with friends, she would sometimes pick up the check, but not always because "it can get really obnoxious if every time we go out I'm paying." She was so thrifty, in fact, that it wasn't unusual for her accountant to call her up and say, "You could spend a little more money!"

"My manager laughs at me because I still shop like I'm poor," Alanis once explained. "I had a meeting with my accountant, who went through some financial projections for the next year. It should have blown my mind, but it didn't."

Her preferred thrills came pretty cheaply. She delved deeply into yoga, taking time to go on a retreat to really study this ancient form of relaxation and meditation. In a stark contrast to the stillness and quiet she experienced with yoga, she also took up spinning, the latest fashionable exercise program and one that involves a rigorous workout on an exercise bike and hours at the gym. And when she wasn't working up a sweat indoors, she went outdoors to take some long trips on her rollerblades.

"She really started getting physical again," recalls Tim Thorney, her songwriting pal from Toronto. "I went to see her for a couple of weeks and she had just bought a new bike, which she'd ride the ten miles or so from Santa Monica to Manhattan Beach and back. That was her thing. She also got big into rollerblading while I was there. When the tour ended, her energy had to be channeled somewhere."

Not exactly the most relaxing of sabbaticals, but Alanis wouldn't have had it any other way. As the summer of 1997 rolled along, she became such a workout fanatic, even taking part in a minitriathlon in Ventura State Park an hour outside of the Los Angeles area. Competing in an event called Mike and Rob's Most Excellent Triathlon, Alanis swam a quarter mile, biked nine kilometers, and then ran five kilometers. She made a weak attempt to hide her identity, entering the race under the pseudonym of Nadine Burke, but her performance was anything but wimpy. Out of the eighty-nine women who competed, Alanis finished near the middle, in fifty-first place, with a time of one hour and ten minutes. Not bad, considering the winning time was fifty-four minutes.

She was pushing herself physically the way she had pushed herself emotionally while making *Jagged Little Pill.* That doesn't mean she didn't take at least a little time away from her unrelenting exercise schedule to enjoy less strenuous pursuits, like going to rock shows. At last, she could go into a club or arena and simply enjoy being a rock fan again. Throughout the summer, she would pop up to catch a wide variety of performers, from folk-rocker Ben Harper to eclectic singer/violinist Lili Haydn to David Bowie. She would occasionally go backstage to congratulate the artists on a good show, but when it came time to do the obligatory record company meet-and-greet picture, Alanis would demurely decline.

Much of the time, she was going out to these events dateless. The relationship with Christian Lane had been filled with ups and downs, and by the summer of '97, it had apparently become just the latter. Their coupling appeared to be over. Her thoughts at the end of the tour about settling down and having children seemed perhaps a bit premature. Alanis had no steady boyfriend, preferring to date around a bit, an activity befitting her status as Most Eligible Female Musician, as voted by Great Expectations, the nation's largest dating service.

The title had little meaning for her, though, because she had come to the conclusion that she still had trouble establishing a true emotional connection to men. They'd always been there when it came to making her music, but not always when it came to sustaining a personal relationship. She always had an easier time establishing a connection with other females, which added a bit of titillating mystery to her sexuality.

"Women are so beautiful," she would explain, "and they just understand things on a level I have yet to connect with a man. . . . There are so many things to experience— I have a girlfriend who's moving down here and we're going to spend some time together, so we'll see how that works."

No matter what she was doing or who she was hanging out with, though, one thing remained constant. Writing. She constantly worked, on her songwriting, usually by herself or with Nick Lashley, but as the two-year anniversary of the release of *Jagged Little Pill* came and went, she seemed in no hurry to commit any of the material to disc. Deep down inside, she could just feel that it wasn't yet time to throw herself back into the whole recording process. "It'll happen when it's supposed to happen," she would explain. "I'm very inspired now. So I'm not worried."

Being away from the daily grind of touring gave her the chance to reflect upon all she had accomplished, and as she gazed back upon her career, she began to yearn for the thing that really started it all. Acting. It had been rather exhausting playing herself, venting her own thoughts and emotions onstage every night. Perhaps it was time to pretend to be somebody else for a time. Even while she was still out on the road, she'd toyed with the idea of getting back in front of the camera. "It takes a lot out of me, singing every night," she admitted in an interview, "knowing there are people listening to things I never thought you could even share with one person, let alone everyone."

Hollywood was certainly ready for her. Several casting directors had started inquiring about her availability not long after *Pill* was released, and were continuing to try wooing her onto the screen.

"I look for someone's sincerity. People like Madonna, Whitney Houston, and Brandy have this genuineness about themselves and their music that they can translate into their

acting,'' according to one such director. "I think Alanis
has this too. I like her. Something about her makes me want
to see more. She's young, energetic, feisty.''

"My interest in her was based first and foremost on my
love of her music and the depth of her artistry,'' raves another. "If anybody has that mystery and that talent the way
she did, you want to pursue it. I'd read about her and seen
some of her interviews and I really wanted to see how that
sense of mystery she had translated into acting.''

The question was, what kind of parts could she play?
It was hard to picture Alanis as the wacky neighbor on
the latest sit-com or the ingenue who must be saved by the
dashing hero in this month's megabudget disaster flick. The
casting directors who were after her generally agreed, one
of them explains, that "she needs to be in a project that
evokes a mood. You'd use her like a Harry Connick, Jr.,
in character parts, and bring her along slowly.''

Still, despite their interest in Alanis and her interest in
acting again, nothing happened. It wasn't for lack of trying.
It was more a lack of interest on the part of Alanis's management, who didn't win many friends in Hollywood by
brushing off the requests. Perhaps her musings about the
subject were just that. Or maybe they just didn't fit into the
game plan her handlers had mapped out for her. Whatever
the reason, nothing happened.

When one well-known feature film casting director approached her management with several ideas, the response
was short and not-so-sweet. "I just wanted to get a forum
with her to see what she was right for, but her people didn't
even ask what projects I had,'' grouses the director. "Their
attitude was, 'Stand in line. She's got a million scripts to
read.' I really felt they should have been more respectful.
I wonder how many things she missed out on because of
that.''

The pull of acting, in the end, was no match for the pull
of getting back up on the stage. After all, that's what had
dominated her life since she was ten years old. So, in early
June of 1997, she accepted an offer to perform a handful
of songs at the Tibetan Freedom Concert on Randall's Is-

Cracked Rear View, sold a mere 2.14 million copies, a fraction of what the first release had done.

"I don't think she'll be thought of as a reference point [for other musicians] until she has a bigger body of work," adds NARAS's Greene. "It'll all come down to the songs. The legacy of Alanis has yet to be told, and the next album will be the key to how she is remembered."

There was really only one way out of this trap. As one of her biggest supporters, *Billboard* editor Timothy White, put it, "the wisest thing to do is remove the element of anyone's expectations and do something very offbeat." It was a strategy that Alanis seemed to have settled upon as well. While the world sat outside her door, waiting and wondering, she was in no hurry to get out there and start recording. What was the point in doing that until she had something to say? And who knew what that something would be?

"All I can promise is I'm going to write exactly where I'm at," she had long been explaining to reporters. "I may lose a few people in my audience. Or I may gain some. I can't say. All I can say is I'm going to be honest with where I'm at. And that will never change."

She couldn't have made it more clear. Anyone waiting for *Daughter of Jagged Little Pill* was in for a big letdown. "I will not go back into the studio to write another 'You Oughta Know,'" she had written in an on-line interview months earlier, when asked about what her next move would be. "I'm a lot more peaceful and a lot less reactionary [now]. But it was through allowing myself to go from being passive to aggressive that [I found] myself somewhere in the middle. As far as what you can expect from the future, more of what's in my subconscious and more revelations."

One thing that wouldn't change, however, was her association with Ballard. Sure, Alanis wanted to branch out a bit and not limit the circle of people with whom she would collaborate. She and Lashley had put together some material. The whole band had pitched in with the writing process while on the road. And she was open to working

more on her own. Still, Alanis knew that getting together
again with Ballard this time around would be a much different experience from those faraway days sitting on that
old couch in the tiny home studio, talking out her life with
the composer/producer until a song eventually emerged.

They'd talked about reuniting, and Alanis left those conversations satisfied that he, too, wants them to head along
paths that lead in different musical directions. "I think we
truly just scratched the surface of what we wanted to do
just as friends," she has said. "There are many things I
want to talk about. There's so much to say. There's so
much to create. And so many observations that I've made
over the last year that I just can't wait to release. . . . So he
and I are not going back into the studio trying to re-create
Jagged Little Pill Part II. Definitely not. No."

There was no doubt about what she wanted to do when
she started writing and recording. The only question was,
when would that happen? Once again, despite all the spec-
ulation, and her publicist's statement that Alanis was officially at work on her follow-up disc, she was still just
taking it easy. There was no way she could go back into
the studio with Ballard. He was busy producing a feature
film, *Clubland*, from a script he had written several years
earlier. It was a movie Alanis could certainly identify
with—the story of a struggling young rocker trying to find
a way to compromise between his desire for success with
his creative instincts in the midst of the frenetic '90s music
scene in Los Angeles—but until it wrapped production,
Ballard wouldn't be doing any recording with her.

By now, it was late in the year. The rumor that a new
CD would be out by early spring 1998 appeared to be nothing but wishful thinking. So, to keep her musical skills
sharp, Alanis agreed to take part in another benefit concert.
This one was an offer she couldn't refuse: the chance to
sing at the annual Bridge School benefit organized by Neil
Young and his wife, Pegi. The yearly show raises money
for the school, a program that educates severely handi-
capped children and helps them ease into society, and is

considered a choice engagement among rock and roll's elite.

The bill is always handpicked by Young, who chooses only the most celebrated names, like Bruce Springsteen, David Bowie, Patti Smith, and Pearl Jam. Getting invited to the event, which this year would include performances by Smashing Pumpkins, Metallica, Blues Traveler, and several others, was even more of an honor for Alanis than appearing at the Prince's Trust more than a year earlier had been. Back then, she was the hottest thing in rock and roll. By the fall of '97, she had deliberately stepped into the shadows and away from the acclaim, yet Young thought highly enough of her work to lure her away from her long hiatus.

Most of the artists tend to perform short, acoustic sets that experiment with new, or at least less familiar, songs. Alanis was no exception. Performing with a three-piece band that included Lashley on guitar, she opened the show with an altered version of "All I Really Want," keeping the song going for about six minutes with vocals that sounded almost like howling. That was followed by a pair of brand-new tunes, "Pray for Peace" and "London," along with a couple that she had unveiled at previous shows, including "Gorgeous" and "No Pressure over Cappuccino." She finished up by covering an old Beatles tune, "Norwegian Wood," complete with the original's taste of East Indian flavor.

Her performance was as intense as ever, and one of the evening's biggest crowd-pleasers. "She really went over well," according to one attendee, who admitted to going into the show as something less than a fan of her music. "She really connected with the crowd."

The reviewers were mixed in their response. Veteran *Los Angeles Times* critic Robert Hilburn was quite enthusiastic about the brief show, crediting her with adjusting to the pressures of her success quite well and avoiding "the temptation to stick to the safe, hit material." The new songs, he raved, "reflected an artist trying to explore new ground.

They did, however, share welcome traits with the *Pill* tunes, chiefly accessibility and point of view.''

On the other hand, *New York Times* writer Neil Strauss was significantly less enthusiastic. In his review, he devoted only one sentence to her performance. ''Ms. Morissette performed several strange new numbers distinguished by a prosaic, Prozac-like facade of happiness.'' He wasn't alone in noticing how this material, which Alanis had worked on without Ballard's assistance, seemed quite different from the instantly accessible music on *Pill*.

''You could tell these songs weren't written with Glen,'' says another music industry executive who attended the show. ''It was very ethereal. I knew from talking to her that this seemed like more her personal style. It was where her head was at the time.''

Once upon a time, critics picked on Alanis for being too angry. Now, she was apparently too happy. There was no pleasing some people, but then, ever since she'd moved to Toronto to start her life and music over again, she'd been determined not to just try to please others. That is why both of these critiques were missing the point.

Certainly Alanis had sung some songs that featured a woman who was pretty ticked off. And there's no disputing that on occasion, her material was as upbeat and encouraging as a group therapy session. To examine any of these moments individually and assume they spoke for the whole person, however, was wrong. Her songs were more like snapshots taken of whatever she was experiencing at a given moment, and her concerts were like a photo album showing off the many sides of the singer. They may create different moods, but they all have one thing in common. They illustrate real life.

As her year off came to a close, and the time to go in and record her next album was at hand, Alanis was dusting off her camera lens without knowing quite what she was going to capture. And it didn't matter. This was what the success of *Jugged Little Pill* had done for her. It had given her a sense of freedom that she was still getting used to exploring.

"That time of my life [writing the songs for *Pill*] happened to be one where I was letting out a lot of things that I had repressed for a long time," she has explained. "So I feel like that was a new beginning point for me. . . . I've written a lot of stuff in the past, but it was all very safe. Because I was nowhere near being as secure a person as I am now."

This was what she had been striving for. She was now writing from a place of strength instead of a place of fear and insecurity. It was new territory for her, and would take some getting used to. At the same time, it was exciting and she couldn't wait for whatever was to come next. "There's not a blueprint for the way I want to live my life. I feel I'm drawing it up right now," she confessed earlier in the year.

That's why all the concerns normally raised about rock stars in her position were irrelevant to her. Would her career be finished if the next record didn't come close to the success of the previous one? Where could she possibly find the inspiration for her music, now that life was pretty damn good? Would she get swept up in the trappings of fame, and drift away from that common bond she shared with her audience? None of this had been a problem for her before, with Alanis making up her own rules as she went, and there was no reason to suspect it would be in the future.

That's because she had already been through stardom and seen it slip through her hands. The experience turned everything around for her, teaching her to look inside herself instead of to outside influences for approval. That philosophy not only applied to her songwriting. It applied to her life as well. And to the lives of everyone who bought a copy of *Jagged Little Pill*. It wasn't easy getting to this place. She'd been through a lot of joy and pain before discovering she possessed this amazing ability to translate personal experience into universal truths. As a result, her music had become a mission. There was no turning back.

Whatever it is that she does next, one thing is certain. You'd wanta know.

BIBLIOGRAPHY

PRINT INTERVIEWS

Abraham, Carolyn and Norman Provencher. "The Song of Alanis Morissette." *Ottawa Citizen*, 24 February 1996.

Meredith Brooks Interview. *The Alanis Press: Table of Contents*.

Aizlewood, John. "Alanis Morissette: She's Got the Whole World in Her Hands." *Q Magazine*, August 1996.

Ali, Lorraine. "'Jagged' Edge." *Los Angeles Times*, 30 July 1995.

Alter, Jonathan. "I Fought the V-Chip." *Newsweek*, 11 March 1996.

Arnold, Gina. "They Oughta Know Better." *San Francisco Chronicle*, 25 February 1996.

Ayers, Anne. "Alanis Morissette: Jagged Little Pill." *USA Today*, 13 June 1995.

Beam, Jon. "Morissette at Ease with Success." *Minneapolis–St. Paul Star Tribune*, 11 March 1996.

Bee News Services. "Gift for Alanis Morissette." *The Fresno Bee*, 14 March 1996.

Benza, A. J. and Michael Lewittes. "Plenty Plush for Pope." *New York Post*, 28 September 1995.

Berger, John. "Morissette Gives Fans Lots to Swallow." *Honolulu Star-Bulletin*, 16 December 1996.

Billboard Top 200 Charts (July 1, 1995–Dec. 31, 1996).

Bliss, Karen. "One Sweet Gig." *Canadian Musician*, June 1996.

Borzillo, Carrie. "Maverick Finds Smooth Going for Morissette's 'Pill'." *Billboard*, 15 July 1995.

Botwin, Michele. "Slow Build Planned for Morissette's Career." *Amusement Business*, 23 October 1995.

Brown, Mark. "The Jagged Edge of Fame." *Edmonton Journal*, 2 August 1996.

Browne, David. "Bitter 'Pill': Meet the Advocate for Jilted Lovers, Alanis Morissette." *Entertainment Weekly*, 4 August 1995.

————. "Working the 'Jagged' Edge: How Alanis Morissette Went from Canadian Pop Princess to Alterna-Queen." *Entertainment Weekly*, 20 October 1995.

"Alanis Scores a Hat Trick at MTV Awards." *The Canadian Press*, 5 September 1996.

"Morissette Expletive Deleted from Canadian Collection." *The Canadian Press*, 16 March 1996.

Cantin, Paul. "What You Oughta Know." *Ottawa Sun*, Sun Media. www.canoe.ca, 1996.

————. "Alanis's Next Move: After Jagged Little Pill, What Can She Do for an Encore?" *Ottawa Sun*, 8 August 1996.

————. "Alanis Goes Off the Pill." *Shift Magazine*, May 1997.

Considine, J. D. "Morissette's Songs Sport 'Jagged' Edge." *Chicago Sun-Times*, 1 March 1996.

Cromelin, Richard. "A Changes in Seas." *Los Angeles Times*, 8 August 1996.

Crowe, Jerry. "Morissette's Long-Lasting 'Pill' a Sales Phenomenon." *Los Angeles Times*, 27 October 1996.

di Perna, Alan. "Smells Like Team Spirit." *Guitar World*, September 1996.

Farley, Christopher John. "You Oughta Know Her." *Time*, 26 February 1996.

Fink, Mitchell. "Did an Old Flame Flicker?" *People*, 15 July 1996.

Flannigan, Erik. "15,000 Training Bras Can't Be Wrong." *Mr. Showbiz*, 31 May 1996.

Fricke, David. "The Year in Recordings—Jagged Little Pill by Alanis Morissette." *Rolling Stone*, 28 December 1995.

Galvin, Peter. "Meteorite Morissette." *Interview*, October 1995.

Giles, Jeff. "You Oughta Know Her." *Newsweek*, 7 August 1995.

Gleason, Holly. "Alanis Morissette Swallows: Jagged Little Pill a Great Big Whallop." *Bone Magazine*, August 1995.

Gorman, Kenneth. "Hitting G Sharp: I Remember Alanis." *Southam Newspapers*, 30 November 1996.

Graff, Gary. "Alanis Morissette: Fame in Her Pocket." *San Diego Union Tribune*, 28 December 1995.

Grills, Barry. "Ironic: Alanis Morissette, The Story." *Quarry Press*, 1997.

Gritten, David. "Madonna's Double Feature." *Los Angeles Times*, 29 September 1996.

Hannaham, James. "Alanis in Wonderland." *Spin*, November 1995.

Hilburn, Robert. "The World in Her Pocket." *Los Angeles Times*, 6 January 1996.

———. "Not Bad for a Kid." *Los Angeles Times*, 9 February 1997.

———. "Assured Return: Alanis Morissette Ends Her Hiatus at Bridge Concert." *Los Angeles Times*, 20 October 1997.

Hornblower, Margot. "Great Xpectations: Slackers? Hardly. The So-Called Generation X Turns Out to Be Full of Go-Getters Who Are Just Doing It—But Their Way." *Time*, 9 June 1997.

Howell, Peter. "The Real Deal on Alanis Morissette." *Addicted to Noise/Music News of the World*, www.addict.com/MNOT, 13 August 1995.

———. "Alanis: With Grammy and Juno Nominations Galor and 8.5 Million Albums Sold Around the World, This Canadian Rules Alternative Rock." *Southam Newspapers*, 24 February 1996.

Janssen, Jan. "Alanis Morissette." Australian *Playboy*, July 1997.

Jennings, Nicholas. "The Adventures of Alanis in Wonderland." *MacLean's*, 11 December 1995.

Karger, Dave. "Defining Moment." *Entertainment Weekly*, 19 April 1996.

Lai, Annette M. "Alanis Morissette: Jagged Little Pill." *Gavin Report*, June 1995.

LeBlanc, Larry. "Alexander Tousts Canadian Ties at MCA." *Billboard*, 1 August 1992.

———. "Junos Swept by Morissette." *Billboard*, 23 March 1996.

Livingstone, Barb. "Critic Abandons Job for Pop Star." *Calgary Herald*, 16 November 1992.

Luscombe, Belinda. "Seen and Heard." *Time*, 25 March 1996.

"Presenting a Jagged Little Key." *MacLean's*, 4 March 1996.

MacDonald, Marianne. "Alanis Plans a Painting Party." Scripps-Howard News Service, 30 September 1997.

Moon, Tom. "Alanis Is All the Rage." Knight-Ridder Newspapers, 16 November 1995.

Morse, Steve. "He Oughta Know." *The Boston Globe*, 31 March 1996.

Muretich, James. "It's Like . . . Wow! I Love It!" *Calgary Herald*, 11 July 1991.

"Dean Cain, Brad Pitt Top List of Most Eligible Celebrities." *Mr. Showbiz*, 4 December 1996.

Naylor, Janet. "Canadian Recounts Antics for Full House." *Detroit News*, 7 May 1997.

Nicholls, Stephen. "Ottawa Teen Riding High." *The Canadian Press*, 6 November 1992.

"Juno Postcard." *Ottawa Sun*, March 1992.

"What People Earn." *Parade*, 22 June 1997.

Pareles, Jon. "Alanis Morissette Review: Tramps, New York City." *New York Times*, 18 August 1995.

————. "Alanis Morissette: Better to Sing the Teen-Age Life Than Live It." *New York Times*, 28 February 1996.

————. "Rookies Win Big at Grammys." *New York Times*, 29 February 1996.

"Coming of Age: This Time Around, Women Put the Whammy in Grammy." *People*, 4 March 1996.

"Alanis Morissette: A Canadian Maverick Bleeps Her Way to a Place in Pop History." *People*, 30 December 1996.

"Alanis Morissette on the Jagged Little Pill, Live Home Video Set for Release," July 1 Press Release.

Raphael, Amy. "Look at Me, I'm Famous." *Manchester Guardian*, 10 October 1995.

Rhodes, Joe. "Doing It His Way." *Cigar Afficionado*, Summer 1996.

Rogers, Dave. "Local Man Pushes for Recognition of City's 'Icon.' " *Ottawa Citizen*, 21 May 1997.

Rogers, Kalen. "The Story of Alanis Morissette." *Omnibus Press*, 1996.

Ross, Mike. "Alanis Snubbed an Early Benefactor." *Edmonton Sun: Express*, 26 September 1997.

Sakamoto, John. "Alanis's New Songs." *Jam! Showbiz*, 8 August 1996.

Smith, Ethan. "It Takes Two." *Entertainment Weekly*, 11 October 1996.

Snyder, Michael. "Morissette Burns on American Tour." *San Francisco Chronicle*, 17 July 1995.

Spurrier, Jeff. "The People's Courtney." *Details*, October 1995.

Stevenson, Jane. "Morissette Riding High in Polls." *Toronto Sun*, 8 January 1996.

Stewart, Allison. "Morissette Lends Her Voice to a Hungry Generation." *Chicago Tribune*, 3 September 1996.

Strauss, Neil. "New Faces in Grammy Nominations." *New York Times*, 5 January 1996.

———. "Alanis Morissette Review: Roseland, New York City." *New York Times*, 8 February 1996.

———. "Neil Young and Friends: This Benefit's for Real." *New York Times*, 20 October 1997.

Sutcliffe, Phil. "The Ever-Popular Tortured Artist Effect." *Mojo*, July 1996.

————. "Behind Every Great Woman." August 1996.

Taylor, Kim. "My 15 Minutes with Alanis." *Hypno*, Vol. 5, Issue 3.

White, Timothy. "Music to My Ears: Morissette's Jagged Self-Healing." *Billboard*, 13 May 1995.

Wild, David. "The Adventures of Miss Thing." *Rolling Stone*, 2 November 1995.

Willman, Chris. "Quiet Riot Grrrl." *Entertainment Weekly*, 15 March 1996.

————. "'96 Tears: Music Winners and Losers." *Entertainment Weekly*, 17 January 1997.

RADIO AND ON-LINE INTERVIEWS

KPOI, 97.5. Honolulu, HI, 6 August 1995.

WENZ, 107.9. Cleveland, OH, 20 August 1995.

WHTZ, 100.3. New York, NY, 15 August 1995.

WNEW, 102.7. New York, NY, 15 August 1995.

Channel 3 News. Auckland, New Zealand, 13 December 1996.

America On-Line, 1996.

MTV News, June 1997.

VIDEOS

Jagged Little Pill, Live. Warner Reprise Video, 1997.

Just One of the Girls. Saban Entertainment, 1993.

New Year's Eve: Niagra Falls. Baton Broadcasting System, 1993.